LEO NAJO: Baseball's First Latino Superstar

By Noe Torres

With an Afterword by Athit Farias, Leo Najo's Granddaughter

Edinburg, Texas

© 2020 Noe Torres

Originally published as *Baseball's First Mexican American Star: The Amazing Story of Leo Najo* (2005).

All rights reserved. No part of this publication may be reproduced or transmitted in any form or by any means electronic or mechanical, including photocopy, recording, or any information storage and retrieval system, without permission in writing from both the copyright owner and the publisher.

ISBN: 978-0-9817597-3-9

Printed in the United States of America

PCN

Dedication

To my wife Robin and daughter Sarah, who, though they do not understand my obsession with baseball, have learned to indulge me. Moreover, for my son Stephen, who gave me a whole new perspective on baseball using his game console.

Special Thanks

This book could not have been written without the support and assistance of Elida Alaniz, Athit Farias, Alicia Farias, Eliseo Pompa, Pikey Rodriguez, Jose Mario Cavazos, Grace Garza (*in memory of Edelmiro "Eddie" Garza*), my cousin Art Garcia, the Najo Oldtimers Organization, the RGV Sports Hall of Fame, and the Society for American Baseball Research (*SABR*).

TABLE OF CONTENTS

Prologue: The Phantom in the Outfield............................ i
Chapter 1: From Mexico to Texas (1899-1923) 1
Chapter 2: The Minors Come Calling (1922-1923)...................8
Chapter 3: The San Antonio Bears (1924)..............................11
Chapter 4: The Tyler Trojans (1924) 19
Chapter 5: The Okmulgee Drillers (1925) 25
Chapter 6: The Chicago White Sox (1926)..............................30
Chapter 7: Broken in San Antonio (1926) 38
Chapter 8: Return to San Antonio (1927) 48
Chapter 9: Setting Records in San Antonio (1928)...................54
Chapter 10: Omaha, Nebraska (1929)......................................58
Chapter 11: Lower Rio Grande Valley League (1930)............63
Chapter 12: Omaha, Year Two (1930)....................................73
Chapter 13: Omaha to San Antonio (1931)..............................79
Chapter 14: San Antonio to Tulsa (1932) 85
Chapter 15: Fall From Grace and Return to S. Texas (1933) ..94
Chapter 16: The Mission 30-30s (1933-1937) 98
Chapter 17: The McAllen Palms (1938) 109
Chapter 18: The Mexican League Years (1939-1940)...........116
Chapter 19: *El Gran Najo* Settles Down (1944) 124
Chapter 20: The Rio Grande Valley League (1950) 130
Chapter 21: Baseball's S. Texas Ambassador (1951-1978) ..134
Afterword by Leo Najo's Granddaughter 143
Bibliography...148
Index..160

Prologue
The Phantom in the Outfield

On a warm evening in the Rio Grande Valley of South Texas not long ago, Chayo Alaniz walked across the outfield grass of a baseball stadium that is named for her father, legendary Latino baseball player Leonardo "Leo Najo" Alaniz, who died in 1978. Chayo decided to visit the stadium, located in the city of Mission, after hearing reports that sometimes late at night people see a ghostly figure standing alone in centerfield. Local residents believe it is the spirit of Leo Najo, returning to his position at centerfield, ready to play his beloved game of baseball at a moment's notice, even in the afterlife.

Just beyond the outfield wall, a few hundred feet away is Mission's Laurel Hill Cemetery, the final resting place of Chayo's father. A large monument features a sketch of Leo Najo in his glory days, leaping high into the air to snag a baseball headed out of the ballpark.

Chayo scanned the empty bleachers hoping to catch a glimpse of the mysterious figure that some claim to have seen. As she approached centerfield, she felt a sudden gust of wind sweep across her face. "For a moment, I felt my father's presence," she said. "It could have been my imagination, but it was a good feeling."

Today, not many people outside of South Texas remember Chayo's father, and yet he was one of the most outstanding baseball players of the early 20th century. The tale of a young immigrant from an impoverished background who rose to prominence in American professional baseball seems interesting enough. However, the fact that Leo Najo, a Mexican native of dark complexion, accomplished what he did amidst the prevailing racial prejudice and social injustice of his time makes his story seem like imaginative fiction.

Najo was a lightning-fast outfielder who lit up scoreboards and set records wherever he played in the 1920s and 1930s. Born in Mexico but transplanted to South Texas when he was ten, Najo played baseball at a time in American history when the game was lily-white and neither Latinos nor African Americans were welcomed. Given the racial discrimination of the time, his successes as a ballplayer are breathtaking.

Najo was one of the first native-born Mexicans to play professional baseball in the United States, appearing with the San Antonio Bears of the Class A Texas League in 1924. He electrified San Antonio crowds with his amazing speed and astonishing catches in the outfield. In one game with San Antonio, he set a Texas League record by making twelve outfield putouts in a single game.

Najo had such an outstanding first two seasons in the minor leagues that the Chicago White Sox drafted him in the winter of 1925, and he became one of the first Mexican-born players ever taken by a major league team. A November 8, 1925 *Washington Post* article refers to Najo as "one of the greatest baseball players of all time."

When he participated in spring training games for the White Sox in 1926, he was, it is believed, the first Mexican native to wear the uniform of a major league club, predating by seven years Baldmero Melo Almada, who is commonly recognized as the first Mexican-born major leaguer. Judge Kenesaw Mountain Landis, baseball's first commissioner, watched him play in a White Sox uniform that year. Decades later, in 1973, another baseball commissioner, Bowie Kuhn, attended his induction into the Baseball Hall of Fame of Mexico.

Although his dream of finding a permanent spot on the White Sox roster was cut short by an untimely leg injury in the summer of 1926, Najo went on to an outstanding minor league career that spanned more than twenty years. A quiet, reflective, and unassuming man, Najo took everything that happened to him in stride. Rather than dwelling on the misfortunes of the past, he moved on to accomplish the impossible.

His career actually soared after he left the White Sox, and he wrote himself into pro baseball's record books as a member of the 1932 Tulsa Oilers team that has been rated one of the top 100 minor league teams of all time. Unfortunately, the peak of his career coincided with

LEO NAJO: BASEBALL'S FIRST LATINO SUPERSTAR

America's Great Depression, during which the industry of professional baseball, like most others, was in economic shambles. Had it not been for this, he would likely have made it back to the majors.

In 1939, he was in the first group of players elected to the Mexican Professional Baseball Hall of Fame. In 1973, he became the first player inducted into the Mexican baseball shrine. A bronze statue of Najo sits in the *Temple of Baseball's Immortals* in Monterrey, Mexico.

After his playing days were over, Najo used his regional fame to promote the game of baseball for the remainder of his life. An ambassador for the game on both sides of the Rio Grande River, he continued playing, managing, coaching, and umpiring at all levels for decades. Many South Texas residents fondly remember his patience in sharing his baseball wisdom with generations of young ballplayers.

Najo's success as a player is an incredible story indeed. By no means physically imposing, he used his wiry 5-foot, 9-inch frame to its fullest advantage and relied on speed, agility, and intelligence. A former teammate told the *San Antonio Express-News*, "When you use your head, you can be faster than you really are – and Leo always used his head. He wasn't well educated, but he was a smart man. And he wasn't very big, but he had that knack to be able to connect with the ball and hit it a long way."

Najo's story is so unique that in 1975 Metro-Goldwyn Mayer offered Leo a contract for the movie and television rights to the story of his life. Although no film was ever made, the event underscores the significance of Najo's career.

While South Texans still recall Leo's outstanding success on the field of play, what most people remember best about him is his honest, caring, and humble nature. His granddaughter Athit Farias says fondly of him, "He was not just a damned good baseball player, but a very complex and humble man, who loved his family deeply."

Athit tells the story of a day in the early 1970s when reporters from throughout Texas and Mexico descended upon the residence of Najo and his family to get Leo's opinion about being inducted into the Mexican Baseball Hall of Fame. Taken very much by surprise, Najo wept and found himself speechless when trying to answer the many questions directed at him. "I don't think my grandfather ever thought himself worthy," Athit says.

His daughter, Alicia Farias, remembers that her father shied away from fame. "He never talked about his career as a player. He was very humble about that. He was just a normal father to us, and he always made time for us."

Leo Najo Field in Mission, Texas (Photo by Noe Torres)

In many ways, Leo Najo has become a phantom center fielder in American baseball culture. His story underscores the long and difficult road that Latinos traversed before they were allowed to share in the American dream. Underrated, underappreciated, and mostly forgotten by the game's historians, Najo is crucial to an understanding of the important early contribution of Latino players to baseball's history. Not only was Najo a tremendous ball player, but he was also a pioneer in opening the door for future generations of Latino ballplayers who eventually burst through the prejudice and forever changed the face of America's favorite pastime. Najo's amazing

LEO NAJO: BASEBALL'S FIRST LATINO SUPERSTAR

spirit and determination still live today among all those who know of him, and his career continues to inspire baseball fans and players everywhere.

Chapter 1
From Mexico to Texas (1899-1923)

Leo Najo was born *Leonardo Alanis* on February 17, 1899 in the tiny Mexican ranching community of La Lajilla, Nuevo Leon, about 25 miles west of Zapata, Texas. The child of a single mother, Leo moved with his mom to nearby Mission, Texas in 1909, where the family resided in a house on West 7th (now Leo Najo) Street, close to the town's most prominent Catholic church, Our Lady of Guadalupe.

Leo Najo as a Child, Circa 1909 (Courtesy of Alicia Farias)

Why Leo's mother, Rosario, left her roots in Nuevo Leon and crossed the Rio Grande into the United States is unknown. Some family members speculate that Rosario was forced to flee Mexico after it was discovered that she was the mistress of a prominent man in La Lajilla. What is known is that when she arrived in Mission, she brought a fair amount of money with her, as well as a flair for business. Landing on her feet quickly in her new surroundings, Rosario acquired a tavern at 515 South Conway Avenue in downtown Mission. Relying on grit and good business instincts, Rosario turned the tavern into a steady source of income for her and her young son. With his mom's business established, Leo was able to devote a considerable amount of his free time to playing sports with other youngsters in Mission.

Documents at the Mission Historical Museum indicate that Najo attended the Catholic School at Our Lady of Guadalupe Church in Mission. He helped pay the private school tuition by doing custodial work for the school. He also later attended Mission public schools, according to a 1971 article in Mission's newspaper, the *Mission Times*. He did not attend high school, family members say.

While participating with local youth in various recreational pursuits, Najo acquainted himself with the fabulous new game of baseball, which he and his friends played frequently in schoolyards and empty fields around town. Najo quickly proved his worth on local diamonds, displaying exceptional speed and good hitting.

In the early years of the 20th century, baseball was truly the king of sports in both the United States and Northern Mexico. No other sport or public event commanded the crowds and media attention of baseball. In Najo's youth, few other professional sports of any kind existed in America, and baseball was spreading rapidly from coast to coast.

According to the *Encyclopedia of Minor League Baseball*, 52 professional leagues existed in 1910, the highest number since the sport was first played professionally in the 1870s. So far-spread was the sport that even Brownsville and Laredo had Class D teams in the 1910 Southwest Texas League, the championship of which was won by the Brownsville Brownies.

Soldiers, many of whom were from the baseball-crazed East Coast of the United States, brought the sport to South Texas while stationed along the Texas-Mexico border in the late 1800s and early 1900s. Even earlier, in the 1840s, U.S. troops operating in Northern Mexico during the war with Mexico had also unwittingly served as ambassadors of the game of baseball. Mexicans were further exposed to baseball by the American railroad workers who were helping the country build its railway system, as well as by American sailors visiting the port cities of Mexico.

LEO NAJO: BASEBALL'S FIRST LATINO SUPERSTAR

By the time Leo Najo reached his teenage years, baseball had become a consuming passion among sports-minded young men on both sides of the Rio Grande River. Because there were no broadcasts of any kind and professional baseball was typically played in cities far away from their homes, South Texas residents expressed their love of the sport by actually playing the game in whatever venues were available locally.

Leo Najo, Circa Early 1920s (Courtesy of Pikey Rodriguez)

By the age of 16, Najo was playing regularly with a group of adult baseball enthusiasts who in 1918 began calling themselves the Mission 30-30 Rifles (*La Treinta Treinta*), a name taken from the Winchester rifles that were popular then. Though no one might have suspected it at the time, this ragtag group of mainly young Latinoss would become one of the most successful semi-pro teams of all time in South Texas.

The members of the 1919 Mission 30-30s were: Leo Najo, Pepe Barrera, Porfirio Guerra, Jose Saenz, Pedro I. Vela, Joe Treda, Taurino Pena, Jesus Saenz, Jacinto Gonzalez and a soldier from Ft. Ringgold named Myers. Dario de la Garza was the original manager. Over its many years of existence as a club, the Mission 30-30s accumulated an impressive list of players, including future Dallas Cowboys coach Tom Landry, future major leaguer Earl Caldwell, future Notre Dame All-American George Strohmeyer, and future U.S. Congressman Eligio "Kika" de la Garza. A later chapter of this book will more fully discuss the rich history of the Mission 30-30s.

In the club's early years, Mission's big star was Leo Najo, whose displays of speed and quickness on the field soon earned him the name of "Conejo," the Spanish word for rabbit. Taking the form of a chant from the stands, the name was shortened to "Nejo." Legend has it that Latinos had no problem pronouncing "Nejo," but that it sounded more like "Najo" when the English-speaking spectators called it out. Over time, the "Najo" pronunciation stuck.

In addition to adopting "Leo Najo" as his professional name, Leo also began using an alternate spelling for his last name, preferring "Alaniz" to "Alanis." Thus, over the years, he was known by many different combinations of these names: Leonardo, Leo, Najo, Alanis, and Alaniz. For simplicity, the author has chosen to refer to him as Leo Najo throughout this book.

Early in their existence, the Mission 30-30s were no doubt greatly influenced by a weeklong series of exhibition held in the Rio Grande Valley between two of the top major league baseball teams of that era. In March of 1920, the powerful St. Louis Cardinals, managed by baseball icon Branch Rickey, reported to Brownsville, Texas for the first and only major league Spring training camp ever held in South Texas. Also arriving in the Valley to play exhibitions against the

LEO NAJO: BASEBALL'S FIRST LATINO SUPERSTAR

Cardinals were the Philadelphia Athletics under their legendary manager, Connie Mack.

During March 16-23, the Cardinals and Athletics played eleven exhibition games in Mercedes, Weslaco, San Benito, Donna, McAllen, and Brownsville. Although no record exists of Najo having attended any of these games, it seems likely that he and the other Mission players would not have passed up the opportunity to see their major league heroes in person.

Najo played for the Mission 30-30s through 1923, which greatly satisfied his love for the sport but did little for his bank account. "I was making $6 a week in Mission," he later recalled.

In 1921, he discovered baseball south of the border. In the early 1920s, a number of Mexican cities hosted semi-pro teams that played mostly on Sundays. The Mexican professional baseball league was organized and began playing more or less on a full-time basis in 1926.

Leo Najo (left) Playing with Monterrey in 1922

Sports promoters in Mexico, eager to profit from the rising public demand for baseball games, sought out new sources of talent, especially players from the United States. "In 1921, I went to Tampico to play ball," Najo told a Mission newspaper. "They told me I would make $50 a week, but the manager thought that wasn't enough, and they made it $100 a week. That was a lot of money."

From 1921 through 1924, Najo split time between South Texas semi-pro baseball and the fledgling ball clubs of Mexico. According to data at the Mexican Professional Baseball Hall of Fame, Najo played for Cuauhtemoc of Monterrey in 1922.

While playing for the Monterrey "Gray Phantoms" under legendary Mexican baseball manager Homobono Marquez, Najo hit a homerun for a dramatic 1-0 win over Sonora. The game is still remembered as an early landmark in the history of Mexican baseball.

Leo Najo (center) Playing with Milmo of Laredo.

In 1922 and 1923, Najo also played for the strong "Milmo Bank" semi-pro team of Laredo. San Antonio sportswriter Harold Scherwitz later recalled, "He had been playing with the Milmo Bank team of Laredo, a powerful semi-pro outfit that put overflow crowds in a north side park here called Schwab Field when the Milmos came to town on weekends to tackle the great local semi-pros, the Alamo-Peck Indians." According to Scherwitz, Najo had developed quite a fan following in San Antonio while playing for Milmo Bank, and those fans simply moved with him over to League Park when Najo became a member of San Antonio's minor league team.

Several factors were conspiring to propel Najo to baseball "star" status. First, an increasing number of spectators, including baseball scouts, were being exposed to his talents. Second, he was establishing a consistency of play that indicated genuine baseball skills. Third, he was quickly becoming a valuable commodity for whose talents many teams in South Texas and Mexico were vying.

Leo Najo was on his way.

Chapter 2
The Minors Come Calling (1922-1923)

On March 31, 1922, the city of San Antonio hosted an exhibition game between the New York Yankees, featuring Babe Ruth and the Brooklyn Dodgers (then also called the Robins). Playing in front of the largest crowd to ever see a baseball game in San Antonio up to that time, the Yankees led off with a monstrous first inning homerun to right field by Ruth. The New Yorkers cruised to an easy 12-8 win.

The game served as an indication of how popular baseball had become in San Antonio. After several years of seeing their local club finish near the bottom of the Texas League standings, San Antonians were ready for a stronger team and more exciting brand of baseball.

Brought to the attention of San Antonio team officials in 1922 were the antics of an amazing South Texas ballplayer named Leo Najo. From all accounts they heard, Najo held great promise for them in their efforts to upgrade their team. They were immediately interested and invited him to a tryout.

Arriving in San Antonio for his first tryout with the Bears, Najo was anxious to show the team that not only did he have excellent speed and defensive abilities, but he could also hit very well. When it became clear during the tryout that team officials were not much interested in his hitting, he became frustrated and discouraged. Only near the end of his tryout was he given a chance to show the Bears his abilities with the bat.

After Najo was finally allowed to take a few swings, something remarkable happened. Against the throwing of San Antonio's ace pitcher, Bob Couchman, Najo hit a homerun, two doubles, and a triple. With embarrassment and possibly some racial prejudice mixed in, team officials later told reporters that Najo's hits had come off of another pitcher, not Couchman. In fact, they said the pitcher had been Bernardo Pena, a friend of Najo who was at the tryout with him.

Afterward, San Antonio passed on signing Najo.

LEO NAJO: BASEBALL'S FIRST LATINO SUPERSTAR

Leo Najo, circa 1923 (Courtesy of Alicia Farias).

An article in *The Sporting News* later suggested that Najo was not signed because he exhibited "nervousness" during the tryout. "He had a short trial with the Bears ... but his nervousness kept him from showing much," the article said. To those who knew Leo, this seemed a very unlikely explanation. Always one who kept calm under adverse circumstances, Najo moved on from this temporary setback and continued playing and honing his skills with the South Texas semi-pros and with teams in Mexico. While he remained confident that he could succeed in pro baseball, his main motivation for playing the game was his overriding love of the sport.

Late in 1923, the San Antonio Bears again asked Leo to attend a tryout. He later told the *Mission Times*: "I wasn't too happy about going back to San Antonio, but I told them if they would let me bat I would consider it. The owner of the Bears said they would give me a chance this time."

Given a second opportunity, Najo made believers of the Bears management. The December 27, 1923 edition of *The Sporting News* carried the news that Leo Najo had been signed by San Antonio: "Najo is a Mexican Indian, who lives along the banks of the silvery Rio Grande River a few miles below San Antonio.... Local teams who have played against Najo's team say that he is a wonder in the outfield, making almost impossible catches. As a batter, they say that's the only thing he ain't nothin' else but. Such pitchers as Paul Wachtel, Dewey Marshall, Carl Adams, Slim McGrew, and Claude Davenport besides several others say that he just naturally hits everything they throw up to him. If he can overcome his nervousness after getting away from his native haunts, Najo is liable to be heard from."

With his December 1923 signing by San Antonio, Najo became possibly the first Mexican-born player to enter the U.S. minor league system. Baseball historians generally agree that Najo was the first native of Mexico to make it into the Texas League, which had been in existence since 1888.

It was an amazing accomplishment at a time when Mexicans in the United States were treated harshly and viewed as capable of little more than simple labor. Yet, despite Najo's initial breakthrough, few people could have foreseen just how far and how fast up the ladder of baseball success Leo Najo would soon climb.

Chapter 3
The San Antonio Bears (1924)

In 1924, the San Antonio Bears were hoping to build on the excellent season they had in 1923, during which they compiled an 81-68 record under first-year manager Bob Coleman. Though they finished second in the Texas League to the Fort Worth Panthers, the Bears experienced many successes, including a total attendance of 78,783. Manager Bob Coleman returned for the 1924 season, hoping to lead his team to a league title.

Coleman, a bulky, slow-footed catcher, greatly admired players like Najo who "could run as if they had wings on their feet," according to San Antonio sportswriter Harold Scherwitz. Realizing Najo's skill at drawing walks, beating out bunts, and stealing bases, Coleman named him as the team's leadoff man in the batting lineup for the start of the season.

A newspaper account of the day reveals that when Najo reported to the San Antonio Bears, he brought with him his own "servant," who reportedly followed closely at his heels, carrying Najo's glove, his favorite bat, and his suitcase. Scherwitz later wrote that this unidentified helper followed his master around "worshipfully." Najo's daughter Alicia says that she believes it was Leo's half-brother, Gonzalo "El Tonto" Ramirez, who went to San Antonio with Leo.

The scene of Leo's minor league debut was League Park, located on Josephine Street, south of the Brackenridge Park Golf Course. In 1923, the San Antonio Bears had moved into the all-wood stadium, which seated 7,000 fans and hosted major league spring training baseball before the start of the Texas League season.

Even before Najo made his first regular season start, the city's Latino population was already ecstatic about his presence on the team. On April 16, San Antonio's Spanish daily newspaper, *La Prensa*, proclaimed, "Our city's many Mexican fans should unite with the Americans to fill up every available seat in League Park, because one of our countrymen is on the local team's roster, Leonardo Alaniz

'Najo,' a shining star who plays right field. Let us help him elevate the name of Mexico in the fields of athletic endeavor by cheering him on to victory on the diamond."

On Wednesday, April 16, 1924, Leo Najo debuted in his first game as a Class A minor leaguer with the San Antonio Bears of the Texas League. Playing at League Park against the Galveston Sand Crabs, Najo started in right field and batted first in the lineup. A crowd estimated at 5,000 watched a very closely fought battle between two talented ball clubs. The box score below shows the number of times each player batted (*AB*), runs scored (*R*), hits (*H*), putouts (*PO*), assists (*A*), and errors (*E*):

San Antonio	*AB*	*R*	*H*	*PO*	*A*	*E*
Najo, rf	5	1	2	2	0	0
Fuller, 2b	4	0	0	5	4	2
Rosenthal	5	0	0	1	0	0
Galloway, 1b	5	0	3	11	1	0
Meyers, cf	4	0	1	3	0	0
Brovold, 3b	3	2	1	1	3	0
Gross, ss	3	1	2	2	2	0
Couchman, p	1	1	0	0	1	0
Collins, pr	2	0	0	0	1	0
TOTALS	35	6	11	30	15	2

Galveston	*AB*	*R*	*H*	*PO*	*A*	*E*
Munson, rf	6	0	1	1	0	0
Wisterzil, 3b	5	0	1	3	3	0
Brown, cf	5	1	2	1	0	0
King, lf	5	0	0	0	0	0
Anderson, c	3	1	1	7	0	0
Kearns, 1b	4	1	3	12	1	0
Bauman, 2b	4	1	3	12	1	0
Stumpf, ss	5	1	2	1	2	1
Crumpler, p	3	1	2	1	2	2
TOTALS	41	5	14	27	11	3

LEO NAJO: BASEBALL'S FIRST LATINO SUPERSTAR

Galveston led 5-3 in the bottom of the eighth inning when Najo came up to bat with two runners in scoring position and two outs. As the pitch count reached two balls and two strikes, Najo lined a sharp single into the outfield to bring home both runners and tie the game, 5-5. *La Prensa* said, "Leonardo Najo, the Mexican player on our local Texas League team, destroyed, as if by magic, the dreams of victory that had formed in the minds of the Galveston Sand Crabs."

In the bottom of the tenth, San Antonio third baseman George Brovold hit a triple and then scored the winning run on a bad throw by the Galveston short stop. The Bears scored a 6-5 win, thanks in part to Najo's two singles. More importantly, Najo's historic participation in this game opened the door into the Texas League and into American professional baseball as well, for future Latino ballplayers.

The scoring summary below shows how many runs each team scored in each inning, as well as the total number of runs (R), hits (H), and errors (E):

	1	2	3	4	5	6	7	8	9	10	-	R	H	E
Galveston	0	1	1	0	0	2	1	0	0	0	-	5	14	3
San Antonio	0	0	3	0	0	0	0	2	0	1	-	6	11	2

Leo Najo(right) in San Antonio, (Courtesy of Eliseo Pompa)

On the following day, the series moved to Galveston for the second game, and Najo switched over to left field, where he made four putouts. Though Najo went hitless in three at-bats, his team beat the Sand Crabs, 4-1 on the strength of a three-run homerun by Bob Coleman in the sixth inning.

On April 18, Najo again started in left field against Galveston, and he had one hit and three outfield putouts in a 9-1 victory. A reporter from *La Prensa* called Leo's defensive performance "simply grand" and marveled at a very difficult leaping catch of a fly ball in the ninth inning, after which Najo spun around and threw a strike to home plate, preventing the runner at third base from scoring.

Najo did not have a hit in the fourth game against the San Crabs on April 19, but his deep fly ball to centerfield in the eighth inning allowed the team's slow-running 200-pound manager, Bob Coleman, to score from third for the only run of the game, as San Antonio won 1-0. Najo's sacrifice produced a "thunderous ovation" from the crowd, according to *La Prensa*.

The Bears traveled to Beaumont for their next series, and on April 20, Najo hit a single and made two putouts to help beat the Beaumont Exporters, 6-2. "As he has done all along, Leonardo Najo, the young Mexican player, was brilliant in all phases of the game. He received a rousing ovation from the Beaumont fans, despite the fact that he was on the opposing team, when he caught a fly ball in left field for an out and then made a marvelous throw all the way to home plate to cut down the runner trying to score," reported *La Prensa*.

While the over 4,000 fans in attendance watched Najo's awesome defensive display, a masked bandit attempted to rob the ticket office of the proceeds. Police thwarted the robbery attempt, which occurred during the sixth inning of play, and quickly apprehended the suspect.

Najo's wife, Elida, tells of a funny incident that took place at around this time, as Leo struggled to adjust socially to living and traveling with a team of mostly white ballplayers. Leo was having breakfast with the team one day, and unaccustomed to an American-style breakfast, he was uncertain about what to order. Noticing what one of his teammates had ordered, he pointed to a plate full of pancakes and said to the waiter, "I'll have the same thing." When the meal arrived, Leo proceeded to roll the pancakes like tortillas around his eggs and sausages. Laughingly, a fellow player told him, "That's not how you eat pancakes!"

"Well, this is how I like them," replied Leo, as he continued to devour his food, taco-style.

On April 21, Najo then got the first double of his professional career against Beaumont, in a game that San Antonio won, 5-3. He also had four outfield putouts to aid in the victory.

Najo came through with another hit in an April 22 win against Beaumont, before the team moved on to Galveston to face the Sand Crabs again. Najo remained at left field and hit first in the batting order.

Leo had one hit in four at-bats, as San Antonio lost the first game of the series, 0-3. On the following day, Najo moved over to right field and had a single in three plate appearances, as the Bears edged Galveston, 3-2. In the third game of the series, although Najo failed to get a hit in five at-bats, San Antonio won, 5-1.

Back in San Antonio on April 27 against Beaumont, Leo was held without a hit in four tries, but he did make three outfield putouts in a 2-0 victory. He did much better at the plate one day later, also against Beaumont, as he went 2-for-3 with a pair of singles. Nonetheless, the Bears lost, 4-5.

Najo was held hitless against Beaumont on April 29, but San Antonio won this time by a 7-2 margin. Najo's hit single against Houston on April 30 helped lift his team to a 7-4 victory.

Despite his struggles at the plate, Najo was learning and improving. He was also playing solid defense for the Bears. Having no previous professional experience, his performance in the first month of his career with San Antonio was admirable indeed. He established himself as an exceptional defensive outfielder who only needed to work on improving his hitting to reach major league potential.

On May 2, though Najo was held without a hit for the third consecutive game, he did walk in the first inning, was sacrificed to second, and then scored on a double. The Bears still lost, 2-5. One day later, Najo came through with two hits in five at-bats. After another loss to Houston on May 4, San Antonio manager Bob Coleman, looking for betting hitting from his lineup, benched Najo.

Through May 5, San Antonio had compiled a 13-5 record and held first place in the Texas League. Needing to trim his roster due to player limits set by the league and figuring that Najo needed more development anyway, Coleman arranged to transfer the speedy outfielder to Tyler of the Class D East Texas League.

La Prensa broke the bad news to all the Najo fans in San Antonio: "Since all Texas League teams must reduce their rosters to sixteen players, San Antonio Bears manager Bob Coleman has decided to release the popular Mexican player, Leonardo Alaniz 'Najo.' Najo played so brilliantly at the start of the season, but inexplicably could not continue his brilliant ways in more recent games."

The newspaper continued, "In San Antonio's last three home games, we noted that Najo was no longer performing at the earlier high level, and opposing pitchers no longer seemed to fear him as a hitter. Nonetheless, his defensive efficiency in the outfield has continued, and manager Coleman will likely have a tough time finding another defensive outfielder of equal skills."

"Both the team owner and the manager tell us that they are confident that Najo, with one more season of experience in a lower classification of baseball, will be able to return to the Texas League and be the sensational player that everyone expects."

At the time that Najo left San Antonio, the Texas League standings were as shown below. The table displays number of wins (*W*), number of losses (*L*), and winning percentage (*Pct*):

Team	W	L	Pct
Fort Worth Panthers	13	5	.722
San Antonio Bears	13	6	.664
Dallas Steers	11	8	.579
Houston Buffaloes	11	8	.579
Wichita Falls Spudders	8	9	.500
Beaumont	8	11	.421
Galveston	6	13	.316
Shreveport	3	14	.176

Leo Najo appeared in 26 of the 150 games played by the San Antonio Bears in 1924, which was about one fifth of the season. He had 20 hits in 96 at-bats and compiled a .208 batting average. He scored 13 runs, drew 15 walks, struck out 14 times, and had one sacrifice. Of his 20 hits, he had four doubles, one triple, and one homerun.

As a left fielder, Najo appeared in 13 games, made 27 putouts, had two assists, and made no errors. Although he played so little, Najo ranked in fifth place among the league's left fielders at the end of the season. He also had a number of appearances in right field but did not appear in the league's final individual rankings for that position.

Najo(right) In His Prime, 1920s (Courtesy of Alicia Farias)

Strictly from a fan's perspective, there was clearly an expectation that Leo Najo would remain in the starting lineup for the San Antonio

Bears in 1924. In his 26 games with the club, he showed excellent defense, great speed on the bases, and fair hitting. Although many fans thought Najo's early season successes had earned him a spot on the Bears' roster, it was not to be, and Leo was forced to gather his belongings and move on to Tyler.

Chapter 4
The Tyler Trojans (1924)

After Najo's appearance in the San Antonio-Houston game of May 4, Bears owner Harry J. Benson, a San Antonio tobacco dealer, sent him packing to the Tyler Trojans of the fledgling Class D East Texas League. As it turned out, Najo would never occupy a regular position on the San Antonio roster while Benson retained ownership.

Officially admitted into the East Texas league on January 15, 1924, Tyler was a new market for minor league baseball. The only previous team, the Tyler Elbertas of the 1912 Class D South Central League, had disbanded halfway through the season. The 1924 Trojans represented the first attempt in twelve years to return organized baseball to Tyler.

Tyler's April opening day was a great success, with an attendance of 2,900 paid admissions, which was the league's best. Najo debuted as a Tyler Trojan on May 8, 1924, and in reporting on the game, the *Tyler Daily Courier-Times* wrote, "Local fans got a chance to see the far famed Najo, late of San Antonio, in action.... The boy looks good, being faster than one Jimmy Kitts ever dreamed of being. He can hit and field as well".

Tyler manager Frank "Pop" Kitchens experimented with the roster early in the season but still managed to lead the team to a 13-11 start, much to the delight of the Tyler fans. Leo Najo quickly became a big part of the team's success.

On June 11, playing at Trojan Park against the Texarkana Twins, Leo hit for the "cycle," and he also stole three bases in a single inning! The local paper reported, "Najo was the shining light of the game, getting a single, double, triple and a home run out of five times up. He also stole second, third and home base in one inning." Such incredible feats by a single player had never before been witnessed in Tyler, and thus, his legend grew. The statistics from this landmark game in Najo's career are as follows:

	1	2	3	4	5	6	7	8	9	-	R	H
Texarkana	0	2	1	0	0	0	0	0	2	-	5	10
Tyler	0	3	2	1	2	4	1	6	x	-	19	20

Tyler	*AB*	*R*	*H*	*RBI*
Pat Donaldson, rf	5	2	2	2
Joe Longnecker, ss	3	2	2	2
Red Williams, lf	5	2	2	1
George Jackson, 1b	6	2	4	1
R. L. Allen, 2b	3	2	0	0
Leo Najo, cf	5	4	4	4
George Duddy, 3b	4	3	3	1
Pop Kitchens, c	3	1	1	1
Clarence Fields, c	0	0	0	0
Milber Porter, p	5	1	2	2
TOTALS	39	19	20	14

Texarkana	*AB*	*R*	*H*	*RBI*
Omare Kile, cf	5	0	1	1
Hub Northen, 1b	3	1	1	0
Walker, 1b	2	0	0	0
Homer Peel, 3b	4	0	2	0
Smead Jolley, rf	4	1	1	0
Clarence Blair, lf	4	0	1	0
Adolf Krauss, c	4	1	1	0
Wes. Bradshaw, 2b	4	1	1	2
Taylor Phelps, ss	4	1	2	0
C.M. Matthews, p	2	0	0	0
Davis, p	1	0	0	0
TOTALS	37	5	10	3

Errors: Allen 2, Jolley, Peel, Duddy.
Double Plays: Tyler 3, Texarkana 1.
Left-on-base: Tyler 7, Texarkana 5.
Doubles: Najo, Krauss.

LEO NAJO: BASEBALL'S FIRST LATINO SUPERSTAR

Triples: Najo.
Homeruns: Bradley (2nd inning off Porter, 1 on, 2 out), Donaldson (4th inning off Matthews, 0 on, 0 out), Najo (6th inning off Matthews, 2 on, 1 out).
Stolen bases: Najo 3 (second, third and home in the third inning), Longnecker, Duddy, Porter.
Caught stealing: Donaldson.

Tyler's success on the field continued at an impressive pace, as the Trojans raced out to a 29-17 record through June. They went on to win the first half of the split season, finishing well ahead of second-place Greenville. As the second half of the season began, the Trojans resumed their torrid pace, winning their first five games and quickly moving to a 15-4 record. When the season finally ended, Tyler had won a total of 83 games and lost only 37, for a winning percentage of .692. The team thus assured itself an outright league championship, without having to participate in a playoff.

Team	*W*	*L*	*Pct*	*GB*
Tyler Trojans	83	37	.692	--
Greenville Hunters	71	50	.587	12 ½
Texarkana Twins	63	57	.529	19 ½
Longview Cannibals	56	63	.471	26 ½
Mt. Pleasant Cats	56	63	.471	26 ½
Sulphur Springs Saints	56	66	.459	28
Marshall Indians	58	69	.410	33 ½
Paris North Stars	43	72	.374	37 ½

Najo was clearly a major ingredient in the team's success. After joining the Trojans in early May, Leo quickly assumed the team's batting lead. Playing in 108 of Tyler's 123 games, Najo came to bat 392 times, scored 93 runs, made 150 hits, hit 21 homeruns, and compiled a .382 batting average. In addition, he drew 44 bases on balls, and stole 21 bases. He finished the season as the third best hitter in the league. The little semi-pro ballplayer from South Texas had arrived in the spotlight, bringing with him a big stick indeed.

Najo's defensive play in the Tyler outfield was no less impressive, as he finished the season with 242 putouts in 108 games, made only two errors, and had a .992 fielding average.

The final league standings, as reported in *The Encyclopedia of Minor League Baseball* (previous table) show each team's wins, losses, winning percentage, and number of games behind (*GB*) the league leader.

Following the regular season, the Tyler Trojans participated in a championship series against the Corsicana Oilers, winners of the Texas Association, for the "Class D Championship of Texas," also known as the "Lone Star Series." Corsicana, which finished their league season with an impressive 83-42 record, was no match for Leo Najo and the Trojans.

The Sporting News said, "The heavy hitting of the East Texan squad broke up the highly touted Corsicana pitching staff." Behind the hot hitting and outstanding defense of Najo, Tyler won the four of the five games played, by scores of 6-4, 5 –3, 9-3, and 16-2. One of the games finished in an 8-8 tie after darkness ended play. In the decisive fifth game of the championship series, played on September 1, 1924, Najo connected on four hits in five at bats, with a homerun and four runs-batted-in. "Najo, Williams and Kitchens were the stars for Tyler," wrote Marion Barron of *The Sporting News*.

Not only had the season been a tremendous success on the field for Tyler and for Leo Najo, but the club also sported the best attendance in the East Texas League, as 63,000 paying customers registered at the turnstiles. Baseball in Tyler was rocketing skyward, as was the career of Mr. Leo Najo.

Moving on to the major leagues from the 1924 Tyler team were: Carl Yowell, Jack Tising, George Jackson, and Abe Bowman. Despite his outstanding season, Najo did not receive consideration for a move up.

Despite the neglect and discrimination that minority ball players often experienced in this era, Najo was one who kept his chin up and continued playing to the highest level of his abilities. As journalist Mike Finger wrote in an April 2000 article in *The San Antonio Express News*, "Those who knew Alaniz say that one of the most impressive things about him was the gracious way in which he handled his stardom and hordes of admirers. If Alaniz ever received threats or negative feedback about becoming the first Latino to play professional baseball in San Antonio, he never complained about it to friends."

"He never spoke of discrimination," says his daughter Alicia. "Now looking back, I'm sure it was there, but he never talked about it."

Some Alaniz family members say that Najo bore the scars of racism on his body. Leo's granddaughter, Athit, vividly recalls seeing her grandfather's badly scarred legs. The scars resulted from many years of opposing players both deliberately and accidentally stepping on his legs with their metal-spiked cleats while he was running the bases and sliding feet-first. Although Najo never spoke about being spiked deliberately, Athit says that family members believe opponents targeted Leo because of his race and also because he was so darned fast and stole so many bases.

Leo Najo, Circa 1924 (Courtesy of Alicia Farias)

In explaining the use of metal spikes during Najo's era, baseball historian Charles C. Alexander said, "Baseball was a tougher game in the 1930s - a tougher profession to follow and a tougher game to play on the field." According to Alexander, professional baseball was brutal in many ways, as players fought to scratch out a living in a time when opportunities were few and salaries were miniscule.

"I used to look at the bumps on his skinny legs," Athit says, "And I wondered why anyone would endure such pain just to play a sport. I couldn't believe he still loved baseball so much in spite of what he suffered."

His wife, Elida, remembers the many baseball scars on her husband's body. She says, "From his waist down, along the side of one leg, he was like rubber, like a worn tire, from all the sliding that he did over the years. But he didn't complain. He didn't say anything about discrimination. He respected the Anglo players, and they respected him because of his abilities."

Chapter 5
The Okmulgee Drillers (1925)

The San Antonio Bears finished in fifth place in 1924 with a 75-75 record, and some observers might have expected them to add Leo Najo to their roster for 1925. Despite Najo's success at Tyler, San Antonio again passed up the chance to give Najo a full-time job and instead sent him to Oklahoma to play for the Class C Okmulgee Drillers of the Western Association. The Bears did call him back up to San Antonio for a couple of games at the very end of the season, but, because he played less than ten games total, Najo's name does not appear in any of the Texas League individual statistics for 1925.

At age 26, standing 5-foot-9 and weighing 144 pounds, Najo arrived in Okmulgee and found himself in the familiar position of having to prove himself all over again. As it turned out, he was more than equal to the task.

Okmulgee had just completed a tremendous 1924 campaign, finishing in first place with a fantastic 110-48 record. In 2001, Minor League Baseball ranked the 1924 Okmulgee Drillers as one of their top 100 teams of all time. By picking up Najo, they hoped to continue their success in 1925.

Najo got off to a tremendous start in all phases of the game, hitting both for average and for power, scoring runs, driving in runs, drawing walks, and stealing bases. Early in the season, *The Sporting News* noted, "Najo of Okmulgee is showing a clean pair of heels to the base stealers of the circuit, having swiped seven sacks." Before the season was over, he had stolen 41 bases, while also drawing an incredible 101 walks.

Competing against teams from Oklahoma, Arkansas, and Missouri, Najo had a phenomenal year in 1925, during which he led the Western League in homeruns with 34 and in runs scored with 195. By crossing home plate 195 times in a single season, Najo set what at that time was the minor league record for scoring.

In addition, Najo compiled a .381 batting average, with 213 hits in 559 at-bats, including 46 doubles, 10 triples, and 34 homers. He also drove in 131 runs.

Najo Styling, Circa 1920s (Courtesy of Alicia Farias)

He was truly a run-scoring machine for the Okmulgee Drillers, in addition to catching almost every ball hit toward him in the outfield. Defensively, he registered 444 putouts, 81 assists, and only 14 errors in 539 chances. Ten of the 14 errors came when he temporarily filled in at the unfamiliar position of second base, after the team's regular second baseman was injured.

It is quite certain that without Najo on the roster, Okmulgee would not have done as well in 1925 as they did, finishing third in the league and contending for the league title for much of the season.

Back in San Antonio, the team Najo left behind was salivating at the thought of having their promising young outfielder back on the roster. On August 30, *La Prensa* said, "Leonardo Alaniz 'Najo,' the notable Mexican ballplayer whose valuable services are currently being lent to the Okmulgee Drillers of the Western Association, continues to play brilliantly. Thanks to his efforts, Okmulgee is one of the best teams in its league."

The article continued, "In last Thursday's game, the modest young Mexican launched homerun number 34 on the season. Not content at this feat, he also clubbed a scathing double on his very next turn at bat. These hits had much to do with the 13-7 victory by the Drillers over the league-leading Muskogee team of the Western Association."

La Prensa also quoted San Antonio Bears officials as saying that they were trying to get Najo back in San Antonio for at least the final few days of the Texas League season. The newspaper concluded, "Undoubtedly, we shall soon have the handsome young man once again in our midst."

The final Western Association standings, as reported in *The Encyclopedia of Minor League Baseball*, were:

Team	W	L	Pct	GB
Fort Smith Twins	94	56	.627	--
Ardmore Boomers	86	64	.573	8
Okmulgee Drillers	80	71	.530	14 ½
Muskogee Athletics	79	72	.523	15 ½
Springfield Midgets	67	82	.450	26 ½
Independence Producers	44	105	.295	49 ½

On the evening of September 10, Leo Najo arrived in San Antonio from Okmulgee and rejoined the Bears. The following day, *La Prensa* raved about Najo's tremendous accomplishments at Okmulgee, pointing out that in addition to playing centerfield, Leo had also filled in at second base and shortstop. The paper's unofficial statistics showed that Najo had appeared in 150 games, scored 194 times, batted 610 times, compiled a .352 batting average, and made 215 hits, including 45 doubles, 10 triples, and 35 homeruns. Najo's performance surely piqued the interest of the major league scouts, *La Prensa* reported. "It goes without saying that Najo is one of the Mexican players with the largest fan followings," the newspaper said.

La Prensa quoted Tom Connor of the Bears front office, as stating that San Antonio would do "everything possible" to keep Najo in the Bears lineup for the 1926 Texas League season. Connor told the paper, "With Najo … in the lineup, we are certain that our Mexican fans will come frequently to watch our games in League Park."

Najo did indeed return to play in San Antonio at the end of the 1925 season, but only for the final two regular games. Since the Bears had been mathematically eliminated from the league title hunt, team management no doubt saw an opportunity to assess the progress of a few of their most promising players, chief of which was Leo Najo. It was not much of an opportunity, but Najo made the most of it.

Before returning to Texas League action, Najo appeared in an exhibition doubleheader at League Park on the afternoon of Friday, September 11. Najo and the Bears took on the semi-pro San Antonio Aztecas, featuring the pitching of Marv Gudat, a left-handed pitcher who later played two seasons in the major leagues. Behind Gudat's outstanding pitching, the Aztecas stunned the Bears, 8-3, in the first game of the doubleheader. The semi-pro team also took the nightcap, 5-2, on the strength of veteran pitcher Jimmy Brought, whom they had "borrowed" from the Alamo-Peck team.

Despite the embarrassing doubleheader sweep at the hands of a semi-pro team, Leo Najo put in an outstanding defensive performance in the games. *La Prensa* reported, "Najo, the popular Mexican player, participated in both games. Had it not been for his brilliant outfield play, the opponents would have scored even more runs on the Bears. In both contests, Najo literally stole away a number of what looked like sure hits, which brought standing ovations from the large crowd."

In his first Texas League game on Saturday, September 12, Leo started in centerfield and batted fourth in the lineup against the

LEO NAJO: BASEBALL'S FIRST LATINO SUPERSTAR

Houston Buffaloes. He started off the afternoon with a single that drove in a runner from second. In the fourth inning, Najo connected on a triple to left field and later scored on a single by Faustino Gallegos. Najo ended the game with three hits in five times at bat and three outfield putouts, though San Antonio lost the game, 3-7.

On the following day against Houston, Najo made six putouts, and San Antonio won, 5-4. He failed to get a hit in four tries, but his work on defense was superb.

When the season ended for San Antonio following Najo's appearance on September 13, the final Texas League standings showed:

Team	W	L	Pct	GB
Fort Worth Panthers	103	48	.682	--
Houston Buffaloes	87	66	.569	17
Dallas Steers	85	66	.563	18
San Antonio Bears	81	64	.559	19
Wichita Falls Spudders	81	68	.544	21
Waco Cubs	62	86	.419	39 ½
Shreveport Sports	59	94	.386	45
Beaumont Exporters	42	108	.280	60 ½

At the end of the baseball season, the raves for Najo's performance at Okmulgee began pouring in from the national media. *The Chicago Daily Tribune* proclaimed, "Leo Najo, Indian outfielder … is one of the greatest players of all time in the Western association, in the opinion of J. Warren Seabough, president of the circuit. Najo, who played center field for the Okmulgee club, made his first appearance in organized baseball this year and despite his inexperience managed to establish several Western association records. Najo, who was the homerun king of the league, with thirty-four circuit smashes, had a grand batting average of .381." Although the report was inaccurate in that 1925 was actually Najo's second year of organized baseball, it was otherwise correct in its analysis of his incredible accomplishments as a Driller.

Chapter 6
The Chicago White Sox (1926)

In the mid-1920s, the Chicago White Sox were still desperately trying to shake off the ill effects of the notorious "Black Sox" scandal of 1919, wherein eight of their players conspired to "fix" the outcome of the World Series in order to collect gambling money. By 1925, the storied franchise, which finished with season records of 88-52 in 1919 and 96-58 in 1920, was but a pale shadow of its former self.

With eight of its players having been suspended for life following the gambling scandal, Chicago had fallen on hard times, failing to post a winning record in 1921, 1922, 1923, and 1924. In 1925, the fifth-place White Sox finished 18 ½ games out of first in the American League, and their prospects of returning to the World Series anytime soon seemed dim. The team began actively searching for talented players who might help the franchise break out of its downward spiral.

On October 14, 1925, White Sox officials announced to the media the acquisition of Leo Najo. "Indian Rookie, Bought by Sox, Burns Up League," read a headline in the *Chicago Daily Tribune* on October 23, 1925. The article, which emphasized that Najo was an "Indian" not a Mexican, summarized his fantastic performance for Okmulgee during the 1925 season. White Sox officials, probably concerned at adverse public opinion about signing a Mexican, portrayed Najo using terms like "native American" and "redskin" when referring to him.

Picking up reports from White Sox publicists, the *Washington Post* on November 8, 1925 ran a story in which Najo was identified as an Indian despite his Mexican-sounding surname:

"That the Chicago White Sox are trying to get together a team of 'native Americans' becomes more and more apparent as they continue to recruit taken from among the noble Redmen. With the signing of Najo Alaniz, who passes for Indian although his cognomen [surname] would indicate a Mexican origin, they will have four 'natives' on the roster for next season.... According to President J. Warren Seabough of the Western association he is 'one of the greatest baseball players of all time.' He is no mastodon as to size, standing 5 feet 9 and weighing 155 pounds, but what there is of him is all grit, speed and stamina. He has time to develop, being only 24 years old.

"Alaniz played center field, second base and short stop for the Okmulgee team last summer. He was in 150 games and set a bunch of records for the association. Among other feats credited to him are 46 two baggers, 10 triples and 34 homeruns. He stole 41 bases and proved that he could wait by drawing 101 bases on balls besides batting in 131 runs. His fielding shows that he had only 14 errors in 539 chances.

"It was his first season in organized ball and perhaps President Seabough is right, which would be an awful joke on the scouts who overlooked him, as the Sox got him out of the grab bag in the draft."

The White Sox, whose poor team batting contributed to their fifth place finish in 1925, were in desperate need of better hitting, and many observers felt that Najo, the homerun champion of the Western Association, was exactly what was needed to solve the team's lack of power. "The thing may be solved by a Mexican Indian, Lee Najo, who was obtained from San Antonio," said a report in the *Chicago Daily Tribune* on December 15, 1925. "The young redskin played at Okmulgee in the Western association last summer. He is only 23 years of age, but the things he did out in the wide-open country were away above normal. Just listen to this: In 139 games he batted .353. He scored 193 runs, hit 40 two baggers, 11 triples, and 34 homers, and stole 39 bases."

In the December 19, 1925 edition of the *Washington Post*, a sports headline read, "Najo Boasts Rapid Rise in Game: Indian Outfielder, One Year in Minors, Is Signed by Chisox." The article went on to say, "Carrying with him several records captured in the Western association, Leo Najo, who was the Okmulgee Drillers' most spectacular ball player last season, finds himself shot into the big league at the end of his first year in organized baseball. Scouts for the Chicago White Sox watched Najo, an Indian, in action, and later took him. He was owned by the San Antonio club but farmed out to Okmulgee. Speedy in the outer gardens, accurate with his throwing arm, dangerous at bat and always fast on the bases, the lithe young athlete built up a record in the Western association that will remain for some time, J.W. Seabough, president of the association, predicted."

Najo's Legs Show Scars, 1920s (Courtesy of Alicia Farias)

LEO NAJO: BASEBALL'S FIRST LATINO SUPERSTAR

On December 26, 1925, the *Chicago Daily Tribune* expanded on the Indian theme for Najo: "Possibly the most singular thing about the list [of prospective players] is that three of the men are Indians. In the past, most pilots have found it more than a man's sized job to manage one redskin. Two of the aborigines are pitchers…. The third Indian is Leo Najo, a hard hitter drafter from San Antonio, Tex. He is an outfielder, but also plies his trade at shortstop and may get a chance to display himself at that post."

On February 25, 1926, *The Sporting News* announced that the White Sox had claimed Leo Najo. He was scheduled to report to the club's spring training camp at Shreveport, Louisiana.

Spring training began with a team dinner in Shreveport on Sunday, February 28, 1926. According to news accounts, fourteen members of the team arrived from Chicago in special train cars at 10:30 a.m. on that same day and were met at the station by over a thousand baseball fans. The White Sox team members who arrived on the 28th were identified as: Eddie Collins, Ben Egan, Spencer Harris, John Garabowski, Ray Schalk, Clyde Crouse, Urban Faber, Alfonse Thomas, Dick Kraft, Tom Gully, Jimmy Walf, Matty Mathews, Bill Hunnefield, and Bill Carney.

The team's preparations for the season began with a 90-minute workout on Monday, March 1 under the watchful eye of manager Eddie Collins. Players stretched and ran through light, informal drills. Reports of the first day's workout show that Leo Najo did not attend the session.

On the second day of training, March 2, *Chicago Daily Tribune* reporter James Crusinberry noted, "the camp today was increased by the arrival of five more players – Catcher Harry McCurdy, Pitchers Milton Steengrafe, Dixie Leverette, and George Borman, and Outfielder Lee Najo." Crusinberry added, "Lee Najo is a Mexican Indian from Texas. That should give him a decided advantage over ordinary athletes. He's an expert foot runner. When a boy on the plains, he loped after jack rabbits. When he steals a base, he looks like a fleeting shadow. He stole all the bases they had in Oklahoma last year. When he goes after a fly ball, he goes. And he is a socking demon with the stick. He knocked the cover off two balls in practice today."

On March 3, a cold front moved through Shreveport, dropping temperatures dramatically, and the White Sox hosted a visit from the legendary Kenesaw Mountain Landis, Major League Baseball's first commissioner. Landis, the man who helped restore the nation's confidence in its national game after the White Sox gambling scandal of 1919, arrived in Shreveport from New Orleans for a brief inspection of Chicago's training camp.

In honor of Landis, White Sox manager Eddie Collins staged a five-inning intrasquad game between a team managed by Collins ("the Collins Colts") and a squad managed by Coach Ben Egan ("the Egan Eggs"). Playing in the outfield for Egan's team was Leo Najo of Mission, Texas. Leaning his chin on a walking stick, Commissioner Landis watched with interest as the game unfolded.

Reporter Crusinberry wrote, "Senor Najo, pronounced Naho, almost won the game for the Egans in the fifth when, with two on and two out, he pulled a drive over the left wall. The ball was foul by a few yards." The exhibition game ended in a 3-3 tie.

On March 4, a driving rain began to fall in Shreveport, causing the curtailing of many of the scheduled training activities. Leo Najo later told reporters in Mission, "In one exhibition game with the White Sox in Shreveport, they put me in the game in the fifth inning. It started raining that same inning, and it rained for five days."

On March 5, players participated in limited drills, focusing mainly on batting, but on the following day, a steady rainfall turned the baseball park into a quagmire, and all practice sessions were cancelled. Crusinberry reported that most White Sox players spent their day at a card table playing bridge.

Sunday March 7 was to be a day off for the players, but when the day dawned sunny and dry, manager Collins scheduled afternoon drills, including another intrasquad contest. Although there is no mention of Najo having participated, it is likely that he did play in the game, which the Collins Colts won 5-2. The excellent weather continued for the next few days, as the team held full-day workouts, in preparation for the first "real" exhibition game on March 13.

Saturday, March 13, was another unseasonably cold day, with even a few snowflakes falling on the field, as the White Sox took on the Shreveport Sports of the Class A Texas League. Leo Najo played

LEO NAJO: BASEBALL'S FIRST LATINO SUPERSTAR

left field in the game, making two outfield putouts and batting twice without a hit. Najo came up to the plate in the second inning with runners at first and third and two outs in the inning, but he was unable to connect. Chicago lost 0-2 to the Shreveport Sports.

The second exhibition game between the two teams, scheduled for March 14, was cancelled due to a very rare weather event in Shreveport: snow. On the 15th, with the snow melted and forgotten, the White Sox resumed their spring training drills.

On March 16, in an intrasquad game, Leo Najo came up to bat with runners at first and second, and this time he whacked a single to score both runners. After the practice game, Najo was announced as a probable outfield starter for the March 17 exhibition game against the Shreveport Sports.

On the day of the Shreveport game, however, Najo did not start and appeared in the game only once, as a pinch hitter. He made it on base and ended up scoring one of the seven runs scored by Chicago in the 7-0 victory over Shreveport.

On March 19-21, the White Sox broke up into two squads; one traveled to Fort Worth for a three-game series against the Fort Worth Panthers of the Texas League, while the other team, including Najo, stayed in Shreveport to play the Sports again. The Sox beat Shreveport 1-0 on March 20, thanks to a towering homerun in the first inning by Leo Najo. A second game scheduled for March 21 was rained out.

The split squads came back together in Shreveport on March 22 to begin preparing for their next set of exhibition games, to be played in Texarkana and then Dallas. Playing against the Texarkana Twins of the Class D East Texas League on March 24, Najo again had an excellent outing, starting at left field in the game. He hit a double and scored a run in three trips to the plate, and he had two outfield putouts. Najo led the White Sox to a 14-10 rout of Texarkana.

On March 25, the day after Najo's fine performance against Texarkana, manager Eddie Collins met with reporters to announce the names of the 26 players most likely to remain with the White Sox after spring training ended. Najo was not one of the 26 listed. Limited to carrying only six outfielders into the start of the regular season, Collins announced that he had chosen Johnny Mostil, Bibb Falk,

Spencer Harris, Bill Barrett, Tom Gulley, and Pat Veltman. All the outfielders chosen by Collins had previous major league experience, except for Pat Veltman, a rookie like Najo. Possibly the reason that Veltman was chosen over Najo, other than racial considerations and the San Antonio club's desire to have Najo back, was the fact that Veltman had performed well both as an infielder and an outfielder, whereas, Najo was more of a natural outfielder.

In a three-game series against the Dallas Steers of the Texas League on March 26-28, Najo appeared only briefly in the final game of the series, recording one putout at centerfield but taking no at-bats. His time with the White Sox was winding down.

In a March 29 game against the St. Louis Cardinals, Najo was denied the chance to appear in the lineup against the major league team. On March 30, in what Najo may have viewed as another bad omen, the city of Dallas was blanketed by a rare snowfall. *Daily Tribune* reporter Crusinberry wrote, "Several of our players are under a nervous strain because they expect the squad to be cut down by about five or six men about the end of this week, which means that some of the fellows will have to go back to the bushes and eat ham and beans."

Two days later, the axe fell on Najo's major league dreams. The *Chicago Daily Tribune* reported, "The Sox squad was cut down by one today when Najo, the Mexican Indian, was shipped to the San Antonio club to which he has been released outright. There are others tonight awaiting the signal to move."

The exact reason behind Najo's release by Chicago has been the subject of much speculation over the years. Some observers have suggested that San Antonio negotiated with the White Sox to get Leo back in the Alamo City, where his immense popularity among Latinos translated into excellent gate receipts for the team. Proponents of this theory say that San Antonio actively worked to have Najo released back to them and that the team's efforts finally paid off right before the start of the major league season in Chicago.

In a 1971 article in the McAllen newspaper, Bill Walsh states that coming out of Chicago's spring training camp, Najo was listed as the team's fourth outfielder. Najo was expected to make the trip north to the Windy City for the start of the season, but his tremendous gate appeal back in San Antonio set into motion a furious effort by the Bears' management to convince the White Sox that they could hold off on adding Najo to their full-time roster for at least one more year.

Apparently, White Sox team officials were persuaded that they could afford to allow San Antonio to keep Najo for one more year before they moved him up to the big leagues for good. Although Najo would be released to the Bears, fans in Chicago expected that the separation was a mere temporary arrangement ... barring any unforeseen injuries.

It must have been a somewhat disheartening trip back to San Antonio for Leo Najo. However, he had good reason to cling to the dream of returning to the major leagues very soon if he continued to do well in the Texas League.

Chapter 7
Broken in San Antonio (1926)

The San Antonio club's leadership had changed significantly since Leo Najo was drafted in 1923. Harry J. Benson had died in 1924, and a group of San Antonio investors headed by Harry T. Ables had taken over ownership of the team during the 1925 season. Ables apparently highly desired that the talented Leo Najo be on the Bears roster as a full-time player. Realizing that Najo enjoyed tremendous success in his first two years of minor league ball and had come close to making the Chicago White Sox opening day roster, Ables was likely behind the last-minute efforts to get Najo away from Chicago and back in San Antonio.

Thus on Wednesday, April 14, 1926 at Waco, Texas, Leo Najo started in left field for Bears manager Carl Mitze and batted in the leadoff position. Waco featured veteran pitcher Oscar Tuero, a Cuban who had played in the major leagues for three seasons. Najo did not disappoint the San Antonio fans, as he led off the game and the season with a solid single to left field off of Tuero. Later in the game, he scored a run after drawing a walk. San Antonio beat the Waco Cubs 13-4 in front of an estimated 6,000 paying customers to open the season in fine fashion. The scoring for San Antonio was:

San Antonio	AB	R	H	PO	A	E
Najo, lf	4	1	1	3	1	0
Gonzalez, 2b	5	2	3	0	4	0
Rabbitt, cf	5	1	3	1	0	0
Segrist, 3b	5	2	2	0	1	0
Golvin, 1b	6	2	2	7	1	0
Phipps, rf	5	1	3	3	0	0
Wirts, c	4	2	2	5	0	0
Flashkamper, ss	5	2	3	7	2	0
Owens, p	4	0	2	0	1	1
TOTALS	43	13	21	27	10	1

LEO NAJO: BASEBALL'S FIRST LATINO SUPERSTAR

	1	2	3	4	5	6	7	8	9	-	R	H	E
San Antonio	0	0	2	0	0	8	0	3	0	-	13	21	1
Waco	1	0	2	0	0	0	0	1	0	-	4	9	2

In the second game of the Waco series on April 15, San Antonio trailed by two runs in the bottom of the ninth inning, when Bears pinch hitter Joe Henzes led off with a double, and then Najo drew a walk. San Antonio second baseman Eusebio Gonzalez hit a single, scoring Henzes, but that was the Bears' only run, and they lost, 6-7.

The next game of the series was played before more than 5,000 fans in San Antonio's League Park on Friday, April 16. Najo scored the game's first run when he led off the bottom of the first with a strong single to left, advanced to second on a fly ball, moved to third on a ground out, and then stole home. Trailing 5-4 in the final inning with a runner at first base, Najo lifted a long fly ball to centerfield that almost left the park, but it was caught, and San Antonio lost.

In the final game of the Waco series, Najo and San Antonio won by a score of 4-2, although Leo went hitless in three trips to the plate.

Najo and the Bears next moved on to Houston, where San Antonio captured the first game, 4-1. The scoring by innings was:

	1	2	3	4	5	6	7	8	9	-	R	H	E
San Antonio	0	0	0	1	0	0	0	0	3	-	4	9	0
Houston	0	0	0	0	0	0	0	0	0	-	1	6	0

Najo hit his first homerun of the season in the second game of the three-game set. His two-run shot in the fifth inning led the Bears to a 2-1 victory.

	1	2	3	4	5	6	7	8	9	-	R	H	E
San Antonio	0	0	0	0	2	0	0	0	0	-	2	6	0
Houston	0	0	0	0	0	1	0	0	0	-	1	12	2

Leo had four outfield putouts in a 2-1 loss to Houston on April 20. According to *La Prensa*, Najo "played brilliantly in centerfield, snagging four fly balls that came his way, but he had little luck in the batter's box."

On April 21 in Beaumont, Najo sat out a game won by San Antonio, 14-9. Beaumont came back the following day to beat the Bears by the exact same score. San Antonio then returned home for a series against Houston. After suffering a 5-3 loss in the first game, the Bears also dropped a 3-2 decision in the second game and a 5-4 nail-biter in eleven innings.

On April 27, in a home game against Beaumont, Najo had one of his best games of the season. Playing in center and batting second in the lineup, Najo came alive, getting three hits in four trips to the plate and stealing a base, as San Antonio blanked Beaumont, 7-0. *La Prensa* reported, "Najo had a great day yesterday, like a brilliant star of the highest magnitude, both in his batting and his fielding. In four official at-bats, he hit a single, a double, and a triple. He also walked once, and on another occasion was struck out, hitting nothing but air with his bat." Defensively, Najo made a sensational catch of a long fly ball in the ninth inning that would have easily scored two runs and given Beaumont the victory. He received thunderous applause from his fans.

The San Antonio totals and scoring by inning were:

San Antonio	AB	R	H	PO	A	E
Rabbitt, rf	5	1	2	2	0	0
Najo, cf	4	2	3	2	0	0
Klein, lf	5	2	1	1	0	0
Segrist, 3b	5	0	2	1	2	0
Wirts, c	5	0	2	4	3	0
Golvin, 1b	3	0	0	6	0	0
Flashkamper, ss	4	1	1	4	2	0
Henzes, 2b-1b	4	1	0	0	2	1
Ward, p	2	0	1	1	3	1
Gonzalez, 2b	1	1	1	1	1	0
Collins,	1	0	0	0	0	0
McCall, p	0	0	0	0	0	0
Phipps	1	0	1	0	0	0
Owens, p	0	0	0	0	0	0
TOTALS	39	8	14	27	16	3

LEO NAJO: BASEBALL'S FIRST LATINO SUPERSTAR

	1	2	3	4	5	6	7	8	9	-	R	H	E
Beaumont	0	3	0	0	0	2	1	0	1	-	7	8	3
San Antonio	0	0	0	1	0	0	0	6	1	-	8	15	3

After a loss to Beaumont on the 29th, San Antonio came back with an emphatic 7-0 win over the Exporters in the last game of the series. "Najo had a magnificent day," *La Prensa* reported. "In four official turns at bat, he hit three terrific hits that resulted in two runs. He also stole a base and made five outstanding putouts in centerfield, which caused the crowd to give him a standing ovation at one point."

On April 30 in Waco, Najo opened the scoring in the first inning with a monstrous homerun that cleared the left field fence and gave San Antonio a lead that the Bears never relinquished. Najo's team went on to a 5-1 win. Leo finished with one hit in four at-bats, one run scored, and one putout.

Najo collected two more hits in the second game against Waco. But, his real breakthrough as a hitter came in a May 4 game at Dallas, as he went 5-for-5 at the plate, including a double. He also stole a base, as the Bears beat Dallas, 7-4.

San Antonio	AB	R	H	PO	A	E
Rabbitt, cf	5	0	0	2	0	0
Najo, rf	5	3	5	2	0	0
Klein, lf	5	2	2	0	0	0
Segrist, 3b	5	1	4	3	2	0
Wirts, c	5	0	2	6	2	0
Golvin, 1b	4	1	0	8	0	0
Flashkamper, ss	3	0	1	4	2	0
Henzes, 2b	4	0	1	2	2	1
Couchman, p	4	0	0	0	2	0
TOTALS	40	7	16	27	10	1

	1	2	3	4	5	6	7	8	9	-	R	H	E
San Antonio	0	1	2	0	1	1	0	2	0	-	7	16	1
Dallas	3	0	0	0	1	0	0	0	0	-	4	12	2

On May 7 at Shreveport, Najo hit two doubles in four trips to the plate, en route to a 5-3 San Antonio victory. The following day, he launched a third-inning solo homerun to lead the Bears to a 6-2 win.

In Fort Worth, San Antonio swept a three game series by scores of 4-3, 4-2, and 4-3.

Najo's brilliant hitting continued in a mid-May series at Wichita Falls, where he had four hits and one stolen base in one game, and he also hit a single in the another. On May 15, Najo extended his hitting streak with a double, followed by a pair of singles on May 16 and a three-hit game on May 17, as San Antonio swept a series against Waco.

In addition to his success as a hitter, Najo continued his sparkling defensive play in the outfield, and the San Antonio Bears kept winning. By the end of May, the Bears stood at 28-18 and in a virtual tie for first place with Dallas.

Back at San Antonio's League Park against Shreveport on May 24, Najo connected on a double that helped San Antonio win the game, 6-5. He got a single and a stolen base in a 10-7 win over Dallas on May 26 and then went 3-for-5, including a double, against Dallas on the following night. Two singles and a stolen base in the third game helped the Bears beat Dallas, 5-0.

As the season progressed, and the fans in San Antonio became further endeared to Najo, he solidified his position as a fan favorite and an important draw at the gate. In Najo's first full year at San Antonio (1926), attendance at Bears games was 148,533, up from 94,158 the previous year – an increase of over 50,000 fans!

By the first week of June, San Antonio had taken first place in the Texas League with a 32-21 record. Najo had two singles and a stolen base against Waco on May 30 in the first game of a doubleheader. In the second contest, he hit a double and a single. San Antonio won both games. The fans in San Antonio were thrilled at the sudden success of their team, as reported in *The Sporting News*:

"Following the great showing of the San Antonio team, that city has the pennant fever. A pennant fund already has been started with $36,000 as the goal. A newspaper is behind the movement, which got its start when one man gave $250. It has been 18 years since San Antonio has had a championship team."

LEO NAJO: BASEBALL'S FIRST LATINO SUPERSTAR

Najo in San Antonio, Ca.1925 (Courtesy of Eliseo Pompa)

Najo had a single against Houston on May 31, a single and a stolen base on June 1, and two singles and a double in the final game of the Houston series on June 2. He also picked up a base hit in a two-game series against Beaumont. Facing Houston again on June 5, Najo had three singles in five at-bats, as San Antonio won 10-5. He added a single in each of the next two games at Houston, plus one stolen base. Leo was really starting to pick up the pace.

In early June, the Bears front office made a move that was destined to make a long-term impact in Leo Najo's career. San Antonio acquired an outfielder named Frank "Ping" Bodie from Wichita Falls. Before reporting to San Antonio, Bodie had played nine seasons in the major leagues, from 1911 to 1921. At first, San Antonio used Bodie mainly as a pinch hitter and first baseman, but he later joined Najo in the outfield.

Najo continued performing very well at the plate, as well as in the outfield, even as his team battled with Dallas for first place in the league through the rest of June. Singles and stolen bases came frequently for Najo. Against Wichita Falls on June 22, he stole two bases in the first game of a doubleheader and then stole three more in the second game.

The month of July started with a visit to San Antonio by Fort Worth. Najo hit a double in leading the Bears to a 6-2 win. According to Jose M. Cavazos, a Mission resident who has studied Najo's career, the Chicago White Sox contacted San Antonio and arranged for Najo to return to the majors following a game against Houston on July 7. Cavazos says that Najo literally had his bags packed and was ready to head north after the contest.

Meanwhile, according to some Najo family members, dark forces were at work behind the scenes, conspiring to prevent the popular Latino player from moving up to the big leagues. Whether motivated by jealousy, envy, racism, greed, or a combination thereof, a number of individuals in San Antonio seemed determined to keep Najo in town, and the game of July 7 was their last opportunity to do so.

The Houston series began in League Park on July 6, and Najo again played brilliantly, going 2-for-3 at the plate with a stolen base. In the following day's game, however, Najo's plans to advance to the majors were tragically ended by an event that was reported as an accident, although some have suggested it was intentional. *La Prensa* said: "Najo ... will probably miss the remainder of the season due to a serious injury that he suffered yesterday during the second inning of the game between San Antonio and Houston. Najo and [Ping] Bodie ran toward each other at full speed in an effort to catch a fly ball struck by Davenport. They collided and fell in a twisted mass of humanity. The ball fell for a hit, and the runner advanced to second."

Najo, with his slim and wiry build, was physically no match for Bodie, the bulky former first baseman, and the damage that resulted was devastating. The *La Prensa* narrative continued, "Najo's collision with Bodie, plus the fact that Bodie landed on top of him, caused the popular Mexican player to break his left leg below the knee. Najo had to be helped off the field on the shoulders of other players."

In a statement from the team's doctor, Najo was said to be in need of several months of complete rest so that the broken leg might mend completely. *La Prensa* commented, "In reality, this is a death blow to San Antonio's chances of winning the championship of the Texas League. Not only was Najo one of the best outfielders in the league, but he also was a consistently excellent hitter with a batting average above .300. In addition, his incredible speed made him a top base stealer."

Meanwhile, *The Sporting News* reported, "Outfielder Leo Najo of the San Antonio team is out for the remainder of the season as the result of a broken leg. He suffered the injury on July 7, when he collided with Ping Bodie while trying to bring down a fly. The leg was broken mid-way between the ankle and knee."

The "accident" shattered Najo's dream of being called back up to the Chicago White Sox sometime during the 1926 season. "The injury robbed Leo of just that step of speed that had made him really outstanding," wrote San Antonio sportswriter Harold Scherwitz. For a player who relied on speed and quickness as much as Najo did, a broken leg was a catastrophe, and it most likely caused major league clubs to view him as "damaged goods."

According to Leo's granddaughter Athit Farias, after the original injury, a San Antonio team doctor re-broke the leg, supposedly so that it would heal correctly. Najo never agreed with the doctor's action and felt that the additional pain and suffering caused by that questionable procedure might have been part of a conspiracy by certain persons to slow down the rapid progress of his career. Indeed, it is possible that the greatest damage to Najo's career came on the operating table, rather than on the playing field.

Some observers of Najo's career argued that San Antonio had a strong economic interest in preventing Leo from leaving their organization. Najo was a major drawing card for the team, as he commanded a huge following among the Latinos on the city's west side. "Leo was their whole franchise," former teammate Camilo Rodriguez told the *San Antonio Express-News* in 2000. "That team wouldn't have made any money if it wasn't for him. The whole West side of San Antonio would line up to watch him play." Interestingly, despite the fact that his injury was sure to affect his level of play, the Bears showed no hesitation in signing Najo to play for them in 1927.

At the time that Najo went down to injury on July 7, 1926, Dallas held a very slim lead in the standings over San Antonio. On Tuesday, July 13, the Bears had a record of 51-37. With Najo out of the lineup, San Antonio continued battling, and when the season ended on September 12, the final standings were as follows:

Team	W	L	Pct	GB
Dallas Steers	89	66	.574	--
San Antonio Bears	87	70	.551	3 ½
Ft. Worth Panthers	83	73	.532	6 ½
Shreveport Sports	77	79	.494	12 ½
Beaumont Explorers	76	80	.487	13 ½
Houston Buffaloes	75	80	.484	14
Wichita Falls Spudders	72	84	.462	17 ½
Waco Cubs	65	91	.417	24 ½

Team	Dal	SA	FW	Shr	Bea	Hou	WF	Wac
Dallas	x	12	13	11	13	13	11	16
San Antonio	10	x	14	14	11	9	12	16
Ft. Worth	11	8	X	11	10	13	18	12
Shreveport	11	8	11	X	9	13	11	14
Beaumont	9	11	12	13	x	9	12	10
Houston	8	13	9	9	15	x	9	12
Wichita Falls	11	10	4	13	10	13	x	11
Waco	6	8	10	8	12	10	11	X

Number of Games Won by Each Team Against Other League Teams

Although he played only a little more than half the season, Najo's statistics were impressive. In 82 games played, he had 90 hits in 290 at-bats, scoring 60 runs, driving in 24 runs, and finishing with a batting average of .310. His hits included 18 doubles, three homeruns, and one triple. In addition, opposing pitchers walked him 50 times, and he stole 21 bases. Defensively, Najo played centerfield in 68 games, making 183 putouts with 11 assists and only five errors, for a fielding percentage of .976.

LEO NAJO: BASEBALL'S FIRST LATINO SUPERSTAR

If he had not broken his leg midway through the season, Najo may well have made the difference in leading San Antonio to the division title. Unfortunately, that was not to be. Having lost his bid for a spot on the White Sox roster and then having suffered a season-ending injury in San Antonio, all within the span of about three months, Najo's future might have seemed bleak. Few people could have anticipated that his greatest successes still lay before him. The legend of Leo Najo was just beginning.

Chapter 8
Return to San Antonio (1927)

On January 23, 1927, the *Los Angeles Times* reported, "Leo Najo, sensational Mexican ball player who suffered a broken leg last season, has been signed up by the San Antonio Bears in the Texas League." Obviously, a close look at Najo's statistics over the course of his 82 games in 1926, in addition to his growing numbers of fans in San Antonio, prompted Harry Ables to strongly desire Najo's return to the Bears for a second season, despite the previous year's injury.

Wednesday, April 13, 1927 was opening day for the Texas League, and the San Antonio Bears hosted the Waco Cubs with Leo Najo starting the game in left field and 8,000 fans crowding League Park to see the return of their hero. *La Prensa* reported, "Najo did not have much luck at the plate, as in his two official at-bats, all he did was hit foul balls. However, he was outstanding in the field, especially during the fourth inning, in which he made a sensational catch in left field and then threw quickly to catch the runner trying to get back into second base. This play earned Najo a well-deserved rousing ovation." San Antonio won the season opener, 4-0. The game totals showed:

San Antonio	AB	R	H	PO	A	E
Nufer, 2b	4	0	2	5	3	1
Flashkamper, ss	3	0	0	1	5	1
Phipps, rf	4	0	1	2	0	0
Leslie, 1b	4	1	2	8	0	0
Klein, cf	3	1	1	3	0	0
Najo, lf	2	0	0	2	1	0
Philbin, 3b	4	0	2	3	0	0
Warts, c	2	2	1	3	0	0
Fillingim, p	2	0	1	0	1	0
TOTALS	28	4	10	27	10	2

LEO NAJO: BASEBALL'S FIRST LATINO SUPERSTAR

	1	2	3	4	5	6	7	8	9	-	R	H	E
Waco	0	0	0	0	0	0	0	0	0	-	0	5	0
San Antonio	0	1	0	0	1	2	0	0	x	-	4	10	2

In a foreshadowing of what ended up being an up-and-down season for San Antonio, Waco clobbered the home team, 10-1, in the second game of the season. Najo registered one hit in three at-bats. Najo's double helped San Antonio win the third game of the Waco series, 7-4.

After the first two weeks of the season, San Antonio had compiled a 6-7 record and was mired in the middle of the pack, where the Bears would remain for most of the season. Najo was benched for about a week in mid-April. It is unclear whether this might have been for health reasons.

Najo appeared as a pinch hitter on April 25 and then returned to full-time status against Beaumont on April 26, going without a hit in four at-bats. Najo picked up his performance the following day with a single and a stolen base against Beaumont and then went 2-for-3 in the final game of the series. Despite struggling a bit at the plate as the month progressed, Najo stayed in the lineup for the rest of April.

As of May 10, San Antonio's won-loss record was 15-12, good enough for third place in the Texas League. On May 5, Najo had a two-hit game against Dallas, followed by a single and stolen base the following day in Shreveport. He blasted a double against Shreveport on May 7 to help San Antonio win, 6-5.

Najo's outfield play continued to shine, as he used his great speed and quickness to run down and catch many fly balls that other players might have missed. As *The Sporting News* once said about him, "He is a wonder in the outfield, making almost impossible catches." In a retrospective published in 2000, Mike Finger of the *San Antonio Express-News* wrote, "Alaniz's exploits on the diamond once made him an icon among baseball fans at old League Park in San Antonio, where he delighted crowds with his terrific speed on the base paths and his breathtaking play in the outfield."

Though he struggled a bit with the bat in 1927, finishing with a batting average of .295 and only two homeruns for the year, he nonetheless drove in 54 runs and showed consistency and patience at the plate, if not very much power.

Leo Najo, Circa 1930s (Courtesy of Alicia Farias)

Through the month of May 1927, Leo hit the occasional single and mixed in a timely stolen base here and there. He did his part to score runs with well-placed groundouts and sacrifice flies, as well as bunts. Despite his struggles at the plate, Najo played very smart baseball and helped his team in every way he could by relying on his experience.

During May, as San Antonio continued losing ground in the league standings, Najo spent time on the bench, mainly during the last two weeks of May. After returning to the lineup, he went 2-for-3 on May 29 and 2-for-5 on May 31. By the end of the month, the Bears held a record of 26-22 and were in third place.

On June 2, Najo hit a triple against Beaumont, leading his team to a 10-1 win. Still, midway through the month of June, San Antonio had slipped to fourth place in the league standings, and by June 21, they were in fifth.

Some tinkering by the manager in June landed Najo in the leadoff role for a few games before returning to the middle of the lineup. Typically, Najo batted fifth or sixth in the lineup, although he occasionally led off or hit cleanup.

In one of the most exciting games of the season, on Wednesday, June 22, Najo's run-scoring hit in the sixteenth-inning broke a 1-1 tie to give the Bears a victory over Shreveport. The fans went wild as the winning run crossed the plate, and it was such a special win that it was mentioned in the June 30 edition of *The Sporting News*.

By July 5, San Antonio had dropped to fifth place in the league standings with a 39-42 record, despite Najo's continued individual success. On July 1 against Dallas, Najo went 3-for-4 at the plate, including a double, but the Bears still managed to lose a heartbreaker, 9-10. In a game against Houston on July 7, Najo had two hits in three at-bats and a stolen base as San Antonio won, 5-3.

At the end of July, the Bears had fallen to sixth place in the league, and time was running out on their season. Najo was used sparingly in July, appearing in only about half the games. Given the team's lack of success, manager Mitze was released in late July, and veteran San Antonio pitcher Bob Couchman took over as manager. Couchman had known Leo Najo since Najo's first tryout with the team, and following the managerial change, Leo was returned to his role as a starter for most of the remainder of the season. He did sit out most of the games during the last two weeks of the season.

Attendance at San Antonio home games fell by over 60,000, and the team that had shown so much promise in 1926 fell flat on its face in 1927. Despite his team's lack of success, Najo had a decent year on the field of play. He appeared in 122 of his team's 155 games, came up to bat 390 times, got 115 hits, scored 66 runs, drove in 54 runs, had 14 sacrifices, stole 19 bases, and finished with a .295 batting average.

When the season mercifully ended for San Antonio, the league standings were:

Team	W	L	Pct	GB	Attendance
Wichita Falls Spudders	102	54	.654	--	131,385
Waco Cubs	88	68	.564	14	92,755
Houston Buffaloes	85	70	.548	16 ½	144,857
Ft. Worth Panthers	77	79	.494	12 ½	127,427
Dallas Steers	74	80	.481	27	180,129
Shreveport Sports	73	82	.471	28 ½	105,172
San Antonio Bears	65	90	.419	36 ½	88,403
Beaumont Explorers	56	97	.366	44 ½	57,936

San Antonio's record against the other teams in the league is shown in the following table:

Team	WF	Wac	Hou	FW	Dal	Shr	SA	Bea
Wichita Falls	X	11	10	17	15	16	15	17
Waco	11	x	12	12	13	14	12	14
Houston	12	11	x	13	10	11	13	15
Ft. Worth	5	10	9	x	9	11	14	19
Dallas	7	9	11	15	x	9	12	11
Shreveport	8	8	11	11	13	x	13	9
San Antonio	7	11	9	8	10	9	x	11
Beaumont	4	8	8	3	10	12	11	x

Number of Games Won by Each Team Against Other League Teams

Defensively is where Leo excelled in 1927, finishing high in the league rankings for both center fielders and left fielders. As a center fielder, he made 192 putouts in 69 games with six assists, for a fielding average of .990, which was third best in the Texas League. As a left fielder, he made 73 putouts in 34 games with eight assists and only three errors, for a fielding average of .963.

More importantly, Najo came back from his injury-shortened season in 1926 and played consistently and well for virtually the entire season. Things were looking up for him, and, although San Antonio fans did not know it yet, 1928 would be an even bigger year for the determined little center fielder from South Texas.

Chapter 9
Setting Records in San Antonio (1928)

The year 1928 began with a frantic search for a new manager for the San Antonio Bears. Determined to field a better baseball team, owner Harry Ables worked hard to land as manager the well-respected Frank Gibson, who had just retired as a full-time major league player in 1927. A veteran of eight major league seasons, playing mostly at catcher, Gibson had been with the Detroit Tigers and Boston Braves. There was a rumor early in 1928 that Branch Rickey of the St. Louis Cardinals would try to hire Gibson for his team, but Gibson ended up signing as the San Antonio player-manager.

With Gibson now in control, the 1928 season began with San Antonio hosting a doubleheader against Waco on Sunday, April 15. Leo Najo was back at centerfield for the Bears, and San Antonio lost the first game, 2-4, but won the second, 8-2. The Bears went on to a 6-6 start in the first two weeks of play. Najo was the leadoff hitter for the first few games but then dropped to seventh in the batting order, after struggling at the plate early on. Later in the month, manager Gibson moved him to second in the lineup.

The Bears boosted their record to 12-7 in the latter part of April, as Najo found his batting stroke, going 2-for-5 at the plate against Houston on April 24 and lifting a towering homerun to lead his team to a 7-5 win. On April 26, Najo had two hits in three at-bats, as the Bears won 5-0, and on the following day in Dallas, he hit a triple as San Antonio beat the Steers, 11-4.

The April 25 game with Houston was an exciting pitching duel that remained 0-0 after nine innings and was highlighted by a rare triple play executed by San Antonio infielders Ray Grimes and Roy Flaskemper. Najo had two singles in five trips to the plate, and the Bears won the game in the tenth inning.

Najo pounded out three hits and made seven outfield assists against the Shreveport Sports on April 30, as his scoring pace

LEO NAJO: BASEBALL'S FIRST LATINO SUPERSTAR

intensified. He went 2-for-3 with a triple in a 4-1 win over Wichita Falls on May 5. On May 8, San Antonio stood at 15-10 (.600) and in the thick of the race for the league title.

The swift-footed center fielder continued to perform very well throughout May. Against Fort Worth on May 8, Najo went 3-for-4 at the plate, stole a base, and made six outfield putouts to help his team win, 11-1. Three days later, he went 2-for-3 against Wichita Falls. In a game against Dallas on May 30, Najo hit a homerun and a double. At the end of May, Najo's team held third place in the league with a 28-18 (.609) record.

On Sunday afternoon, May 27, 1928, in League Park, San Antonio fans witnessed baseball history, as they saw Leo Najo set a record for the most outfield putouts in a single game, twelve. Najo's amazing performance at centerfield that day resulted in a 2-0 victory over the hapless Beaumont Exporters. A sportswriter wrote, "Najo roamed far and wide to gather in 12 putouts."

June started well for Najo, as he stroked two doubles and stole two bases in a 13-6 win over Shreveport on June 1. Two days later, Najo connected on a double and a single against Fort Worth and had eight outfield putouts during a doubleheader. Doubles and triples for Najo were coming much more frequently than they did in 1927.

Najo had a good series against Waco in mid-June with a couple of two-hit games. He continued hitting at a torrid pace through the end of June.

As the Texas League adopted a split-schedule in 1928, the first half of the season ended on June 29, and the standings were:

Team	*W*	*L*	*Pct*
Houston Buffaloes	55	26	.679
Fort Worth Panthers	46	32	.590
Wichita Falls Spudders	47	35	.573
San Antonio Bears	41	41	.500
Shreveport Sports	39	43	.475
Waco Cubs	38	44	.463
Dallas Steers	32	50	.390
Beaumont Explorers	26	53	.329

Houston, with its first half title, assured itself a spot in the league championship at season's end. For the rest of the teams, including Najo and the Bears, the season was starting over, and they had another chance to win the league title. Najo took on the challenge with relish, starting very well in July. He started the month with a two-hit game against Beaumont, in a 10-2 San Antonio win. One of his hits was a double. On the Fourth of July, Najo went 2-for-5 in the first game of a doubleheader against Waco and then cracked a double in the second game. Najo slammed a homerun on July 6 to lead San Antonio to an 8-7 victory over Beaumont. He went 3-for-3 with a double in a 12-7 win over Waco on July 9 and then went 3-for-4 on the next day. Leo continued hitting well, stringing together several two and three-hit games in the last two weeks of July. Unfortunately, his team was only able to manage a 19-21 second-half record through the first week of August.

Najo went 3-for-5 with a double in an 11-7 win over Wichita Falls on Friday, August 17. He fell into a bit of a hitting slump near the end of August, although on August 28 he had a total of five hits in a doubleheader against Dallas. By August 28, Najo's San Antonio Bears had a won-loss record of 30-33, and their chances seemed slim of catching Wichita Falls (47-17), Houston (40-24),

When the season ended, San Antonio's 35-42 record (.455) in the second half put them far out of reach of the league title. The combined final league standings were:

Team	W	L	Pct	GB	Attendance
Houston Buffaloes	104	54	.658	--	186,469
Wichita Falls Spudders	104	56	.650	1	103,228
Ft. Worth Spudders	83	73	.532	20	119,446
Shreveport Sports	79	81	.494	26	81,920
San Antonio Bears	76	83	.478	28 ½	106,517
Waco Cubs	71	87	.449	33	60,978
Dallas Steers	66	93	.415	38 ½	135,069
Beaumont Explorers	50	106	.321	53	41,551

LEO NAJO: BASEBALL'S FIRST LATINO SUPERSTAR

Wichita Falls, by virtue of having won the second half, earned the right to face first-half champion Houston in the league championship series. Houston won the playoff series, 3 games to 1.

Leo Najo finished the season with excellent statistics. He participated in 158 of San Antonio's 159 games, batted 581 times, got 161 hits, scored 106 runs, drove in 60 runs, sacrificed 28 times, and compiled a .277 batting average. Of his 161 hits, 35 were doubles, 10 were triples, and four were homeruns. In addition, Najo drew 80 bases on balls and stole 17 bases.

Defensively, Najo played centerfield in 150 games, making 423 putouts, 23 assists, and 15 errors. He finished with a .967 fielding average as a center fielder. He also led all center fielders in the number of chances (438).

Given Najo's good numbers on both defense and offense, most San Antonio fans expected to see the swift center fielder back in 1929. Unfortunately for them, their wish would not be granted.

Team	*Hou*	*WF*	*FW*	*Shr*	*SA*	*Wac*	*Dal*	*Bea*
Houston	x	11	15	16	13	18	15	16
Wichita Falls	12	X	12	18	16	14	14	18
Ft. Worth	6	10	X	13	14	12	15	13
Shreveport	6	8	9	X	13	11	14	18
San Antonio	9	6	9	10	x	12	16	14
Waco	5	9	10	11	11	x	11	14
Dallas	8	8	11	8	6	12	x	13
Beaumont	8	4	7	5	10	8	8	x

Number of Games Won by Each Team Against Other League Teams

Chapter 10
Omaha, Nebraska (1929)

According to United States Census Bureau data, in 1929 Leo Najo, age 29, married 19-year-old Lucia "Lucy" Herrera of San Antonio, Texas. The census indicates that Lucia's parents were both natives of Mexico, but she was a U.S. citizen. Leo's family members say that Lucia resided in San Antonio for most of her life, although the census shows her living with Najo in Mission in 1930.

Lucy's inability to have children apparently contributed to the eventual annulment of their marriage in the mid-1930s. Family members say that, following the breakup, Lucy continued to hold a special place in Leo's heart, even after he remarried in the 1940s.

"Leo wanted a family very badly, and he was very disappointed when Lucy did not get pregnant," Elida, his second wife, says. "She tried to convince him that it was his fault they couldn't have any children."

Meanwhile, back in the world of baseball, on January 31, 1929, *The Sporting News* reported that the owner of the cash-strapped Omaha franchise in the Class A Western League had decided to sell off virtually his entire team, after they finished 35 games out of first place in 1928. Among the players that J. Fagan Burch sold off was hard-hitting outfielder Frank "Dutch" Wetzel. According to *The Sporting News*, the Omaha owner "sent Left Fielder Dutch Wetzel to San Antonio for some cash and Outfielder Leo Alaniz, better known as Najo." San Antonio obviously viewed the move as a chance to boost their team hitting average, as Wetzel batted .345 for Omaha in 1928, whereas Najo finished at .277.

Opening day in the Western League was Wednesday, April 17, 1929, as the Omaha Crickets traveled to Topeka to face the Jayhawks. Najo went 2-for-4 at the plate and had two outfield putouts at centerfield, although Omaha lost the game, 1-0. After having a 0-for-5 hung on him the following day, Najo came back in the third game of the year to hit a double, helping Omaha beat Wichita, 5-1.

LEO NAJO: BASEBALL'S FIRST LATINO SUPERSTAR

Leo had a hit in each of the next six games, including doubles against Wichita on April 22 and Oklahoma City on April 28. Typically asked to hit fifth in the lineup, he occasionally moved up to the leadoff spot.

Omaha got off to an 8-10 start (.444) in the league, but the team played a bit better as the month of May progressed, eventually evening their record at 12-12. Later in May, they won seven games in a row. On May 3, Najo went 2-for-3, got a double and a stolen base, as Omaha stomped Tulsa 11-4. The following day, Najo got a hit and made seven outfield putouts in the first game of a doubleheader, a 6-3 win over Tulsa. He then came back in the second game, hitting a double that helped Omaha win again, 2-1.

On May 8, Najo went 2-for-4 with a double in leading his team to a dramatic 5-4 win over Oklahoma City. He had a good month of May, hitting mostly doubles and continuing to excel on defense.

On June 4, Omaha stood at 26-20 (.565) and held third place in the Western League, behind Oklahoma City (26-16) and Tulsa (27-17). Najo was hitting over .300 and making great plays in centerfield. On May 30 against Des Moines, Leo stole two bases and went 2-for-4 in a 9-4 Omaha win that was the first game of a doubleheader. In the second game, he hit a double as the Crickets took an 8-3 victory.

In a game at Des Moines on June 2, Najo had one of his best games as a hitter to this point in his career, as he connected on four doubles in five plate appearances to give his team an 8-2 win. Then, in Denver on June 7, Najo went 2-for-4 with a double and a stolen base in a losing effort to the Denver Bears.

On June 14 against Pueblo, Najo collected three hits, including a double, as Omaha won, 4-1. On June 20, he hit two doubles in a 17-0 win over Topeka.

A day later, on June 21, Leo was having a great game against Topeka, going 3-for-4, when suddenly tragedy struck again. As a line drive hit came toward him in centerfield, Najo ran and dove, trying to make a shoestring catch. In colliding with the ground, Najo suffered a fractured shoulder blade Doctors told him that he would be out of action for at least three weeks.

Najo returned to the lineup in a July 14 home doubleheader against Denver. He was hitless in both games but played well in the outfield, making a total of six putouts. In a July 18 doubleheader against Pueblo, Najo had nine outfield putouts in the second game, while also going 3-for-3 at the plate with a homerun to secure the Omaha victory. *The Sporting News* reported, "Omaha went into second place over Oklahoma City on July 18 by taking both ends of a twin bill from Pueblo while the Indians were being downed. Scott pitched a three-hit game for Pueblo in the nightcap, but Najo's homer over the right field fence gave Omaha the victory, 3-2."

In a doubleheader at Denver on July 21, Najo had four hits in eight plate appearances, including a triple. On July 23, despite playing for three weeks without Najo, Omaha achieved a 53-46 record and was second in the league, behind Tulsa (62-39).

In an amazing game on July 26, Najo hit two doubles and went 4-of-6 in leading the Crickets to a 14-13 win. His recovery from his shoulder injury was incredible. In a doubleheader on July 28, Najo went 3-for-4 with a triple in the first game and 2-for-4 in the second. A July 29 homerun by Najo helped give Omaha a 7-2 victory.

In mid-August, Omaha still held second place in the league with a 66-58 record, as Najo continued his excellent season. Najo started August with a bang, as he recorded four hits during a doubleheader at Tulsa on August 4. He picked up three hits in Denver on August 8 and three more hits on the following day.

On August 22, Leo's mother, Rosario, died in Mission, and Najo made the long trip from Omaha back to South Texas to pay his last respects. Rosario, who had remarried and taken the surname Ramirez, died at age 54 after a lengthy illness. She left behind two children, 14-year-old Gonzalo and 12-year-old Luisa, whom Leo took under his care at his home in Mission. Interestingly, Leo put the name "Rosario Alaniz" on his mother's gravestone, ignoring her new surname and deviating from the original spelling of "Alanis."

With the heartbreak of his mother's death still on his mind, Leo returned to baseball in dramatic fashion on August 30, in a game at Des Moines, Iowa, going 2-for-4 with a double and a stolen base and making six outfield putouts. On the following day, against the same team, he hit a double and a single, and defensively, he had four putouts.

LEO NAJO: BASEBALL'S FIRST LATINO SUPERSTAR

Najo continued his hot hitting in September, starting the month with a 3-for-3 performance at Des Moines. He lit up the scoreboard with doubles and multi-hit games throughout the first two weeks of September. Unfortunately, his individual successes were not enough to carry Omaha into the league championship, and the Crickets ended the season in third place, as the standings show:

Team	*W*	*L*	*Pct*	*GB*
Tulsa Oilers	95	66	.590	--
Oklahoma City Indians	88	68	.564	4 ½
Omaha Crickets	81	75	.519	11 ½
Wichita Aviators	77	79	.494	15 ½
Denver Bears	73	81	.474	18 ½
Topeka Jayhawks	75	85	.469	19 ½
Des Moines Demons	72	86	.456	21 ½
Pueblo Steelworkers	69	90	.434	25

In his first season in the Western League, Najo had seen action in 120 of the team's 156 games. Offensively, he had 133 hits in 421 at-bats for a .316 batting average, and he scored 88 runs. Of his 133 hits, 41 were doubles, three were triples, and three were homeruns. In addition, he had 21 stolen bases and made 20 sacrifices. He finished at number 26 in the individual batting statistics for the league.

Defensively, he appeared at centerfield in 119 games, made 315 putouts, had 11 assists, and had only seven errors. With a .979 fielding percentage, Najo was ranked number 15 in the final individual fielding statistics.

Ironically, Frank Wetzel, the man for whom San Antonio traded away Najo, had a substandard 1929 season with the Bears. Wetzel finished with an unimpressive .281 batting average and scored only 49 runs. To many observers, San Antonio seemed to have made a terrible mistake in trading Najo away.

Considering that Najo was sidelined for three weeks due to a fractured shoulder blade and then missed a number of games to attend his mother's funeral, his accomplishments in 1929 were remarkable. Unfortunately, a dark cloud settling on the nation's economy overshadowed Najo's successful season. Following the end of the

1929 Western League season, the country was plunged into the Great Depression, signaled by the stock market crash of October 23. From 1929 until the U.S. entered World War II in 1941, economic woes were foremost in the thoughts of most Americans, especially those who struggled to scratch out a living in professional baseball.

Chapter 11
Lower Rio Grande Valley League (1930)

The onset of America's Great Depression most certainly was on the mind of Leo Najo at the start of 1930. As banks closed and soup lines grew, Najo must have realized that the nation's favorite pastime was also in for a rough time. Twenty-six minor leagues existed in 1929, but that number dwindled down to just 14 by 1933. In *Bush League*, Robert Obojski wrote, "The minors struggled as never before to survive the lean years of the early 1930s."

Back in Mission before the start of the Western League's season, Leo spent time focusing on his family and on his business interests. The 1930 U.S. Census reported "Leo Alanis" as residing in Mission, on West 6th Street with his wife Lucia, his 13-year-old half-sister Luisa Ramirez, his 15-year-old half-brother Gonzalo Ramirez, and a 24-year-old uncle, Cundo. Najo's occupation is listed as "ball player" and his industry is given as "Western League."

The census also shows that Najo owned his home, which was valued at $1,000. All members of the household could read or write, and Leo's brother and sister had both attended school within the past year. Najo's citizenship status was listed as "alien," but Lucia, Luisa, and Gonzalo were all U.S. citizens.

Following the death of his mother on August 22, 1929, Najo had taken Gonzalo and Luisa into his home. Leo and his family continued to operate the tavern on West 6th Street, which came to be known as *La Treinta Treinta* (the 30-30 Bar). Leo also acquired a number of rental properties in the area, which he continued to manage after his minor league career ended. Leo's wife, Lucy, operated a beauty shop next door to the tavern for some years.

Lucy continued to work as a beautician for most of the rest of her life, even after she and Leo split up and she returned to her home in San Antonio sometime in the mid-1930s. She never remarried and never had any children. When she passed away on February 24, 2004 at the age of 94, an obituary in the *San Antonio Express-News* noted, "Ms. Herrera enjoyed a wonderful life as a beautician and won many hair styling contests. She was married to Leo Najo Alaniz, who was the first Hispanic voted to Mexico's Baseball Hall of Fame."

In 1930, when Najo reported for Spring training with the Omaha team, he did not have to travel very far, as Omaha had chosen to hold its training camp in the Rio Grande Valley, along with three other members of the Western League: Des Moines, Wichita, and Denver. From mid-March until early April, each team operated out of a different Valley city and represented that city in the "Lower Rio Grande Valley League." Each team played a 30-game schedule, with opening day taking place on March 19.

A January 23 article in *The Sporting News* reported that Omaha would train in Najo's adopted hometown of Mission, Wichita in McAllen, Des Moines in Harlingen, and Denver in San Benito. "These towns are located in the heart of the Rio Grande citrus fruit and potato country, near the Mexican border and are within easy motoring distance of each other. From Mission at one end to San Benito at the other, the distance is only 45 miles. Hence it is possible for a club to play at the training camp of a rival club and return to its base in time for the evening steak and potatoes."

The article also reported that the Western League teams training in the Valley received many appeals from Mexican baseball fans requesting that exhibition games be staged in Northern Mexico. "The Des Moines club owner plans a trip into Northern Mexico before he returns home. He wires that he has received petitions from Matamoros, Mexico, which lies across the Rio Grande River from Brownsville, and from Monterey, about 300 miles South of the border, to bring two teams to their cities for exhibition games. He will make an investigation of the interest in baseball on this trip, and if conditions are favorable, he will try to accommodate the Mexicans."

The Chicago White Sox, Pittsburgh Pirates, and New York Giants scheduled visits to the Western League training camps for several exhibition games. The White Sox agreed to face the Denver Bears on March 22 at San Benito and the Des Moines Demons on March 23 in Harlingen. Though the major league teams sent mainly rookies to play in these games, it was nonetheless a thrilling time for South Texas baseball fans.

LEO NAJO: BASEBALL'S FIRST LATINO SUPERSTAR

Mission hosted an exhibition game on March 15 between Leo Najo's Omaha Packers and the New York Giants. An estimated 4,000 people crowded into the Hidalgo County Fair Grounds and watched Mission mayor G. F. Dohrn throw a "golden Valley grapefruit" into the mitt of a Giants catcher, who then passed it around the infield until Giants second baseman Andy Reese grabbed it and ate right in the middle of the baseball diamond.

Najo hit a double in four at-bats, but the major leaguers had too much talent, as New York won, 10-3. The man who ate the golden grapefruit, Andy Reese, paced the Giants with two hits and two runs.

On March 17, one day before the official start of league play, a historic game took place in Mission between the home standing Mission 30-30s and the Omaha Packers. The game is believed to have been the first ever, and possibly only, between Mission's storied semi-pro team and a Class AA minor league professional team. Najo, the South Texas legend, although he was officially a member of the Omaha team, was "loaned" to the Mission 30-30s for this one game.

Mission 30-30s	AB	R	H	E
Barrera, 2b	4	1	1	1
De la Garza, 2b	0	0	0	1
E. Contreras, 3b	4	1	1	0
Najo, cf	1	1	0	0
E. Flores, lf	3	0	0	1
Rodriguez, 1b	4	0	2	0
Tipo, rf	3	0	0	0
Chapa, rf	0	0	0	0
Mape, ss	4	0	1	0
Flores, c	3	0	1	0
Rankin, p	4	0	0	0
TOTALS	30	3	6	3

Newspaper accounts of the day described the game as a fierce struggle between two very evenly matched squads. Mission led 3-2 after two innings, and then trailed by only one run until the eighth inning. Najo had one hit in one official at-bat and stole two bases. Mission actually outscored Omaha in terms of earned runs, 3-2.

However, three Mission errors leading to four unearned runs gave Omaha a 6-3 victory over Najo and the 30-30s.

Omaha Packers	AB	R	H	E
Hetherly, 2b	4	0	0	0
Faber, ss	5	1	2	0
Owens, cf	5	0	1	0
Spurber, rf	4	0	1	0
King, 3b	2	0	2	1
Berka, 3b	2	0	0	0
Senne, 1b	3	2	2	0
Williams, lf	4	2	0	0
Anderson, c	0	1	0	0
Carlson, c	1	0	0	0
Tining, p	1	0	0	0
Railsback, p	2	0	0	0
Malicky, p	1	0	1	0
TOTALS	34	6	9	1

	1	2	3	4	5	6	7	8	9	-	R	H	E
Mission	0	3	0	0	0	0	0	0	0	-	3	6	3
Omaha	0	2	1	1	0	0	0	2	x	-	6	9	1

While Mission was hosting this historic battle, the neighboring town of McAllen witnessed an equally exciting exhibition contest between the New York Giants and the Wichita Aviators of the Western League. Officials of McAllen's American Legion and Chamber of Commerce made extensive preparation prior to the contest. The game was staged at McAllen's newly constructed American Legion Park. "The new grandstand with 2,000 bleacher and temporary seats added will take care of the tremendous crowd that is expected from over the entire Valley," the local newspaper reported. "McAllen's Municipal band will be on hand to liven up the occasion."

On game day in McAllen, Legion Park was described as "taxed to overflowing." In the game described as a "luscious baseball dish being served the fans of the Valley," Wichita beat New York, 10-8, thanks to timely hitting and plenty of errors by the young Giants.

Play in the Rio Grande League officially opened on March 18. In the opening games, Najo's Omaha team crushed Wichita, 7-0, in a game played in McAllen, and Denver defeated Des Moines 6-4 in San Benito. On March 19, the Omaha-Wichita series moved to Mission. Leo, who played centerfield and batted fourth in the line-up, was hitless in four turns at bat, as Wichita blasted Omaha, 6-0.

On March 20, Omaha battled Des Moines in Harlingen. In the fifth inning, Najo led off with a single to right field, moved to second on a bunt, went to third on an error, and then scored on a teammate's single. Nonetheless, Omaha lost the game, 6-9.

	1	2	3	4	5	6	7	8	9	-	R	H	E
Omaha	2	0	0	1	3	0	0	0	0	-	6	9	1
Des Moines	0	0	2	0	0	0	1	6	x	-	9	9	3

Najo finished the game with a single in three at-bats, a stolen base, a sacrifice, and one run scored. Leo's team was off to a 1-3 start in the Lower Rio Grande Valley spring training league of the Western League.

Also on March 20, in McAllen's American Legion Park, the Wichita Aviators knocked off the Denver Bears, 3-1.

Najo scored a run in an 11-6 Omaha loss to Des Moines in Mission on March 21. The game was somewhat overshadowed by the arrival of the Chicago White Sox in the Rio Grande Valley for some exhibition games. The Sox, whose main spring training camp was in San Antonio, started their brief tour of the Valley in San Benito with a game against the Denver Bears on March 22. Chicago won, 8-2. They played in Harlingen the following day against Des Moines. Among the White Sox who visited the Valley in 1930 was Urban "Red" Farber, a veteran pitcher who was with Chicago in 1919 during the "Black Sox" gambling scandal.

On March 24 in San Benito, Najo and the Packers defeated the Denver Bears, 10-4. Then, on the following day, the same two teams played a much more exciting game in Mission. Najo, starting in centerfield and batting fifth in the lineup, scored two runs, stole a base, and collected one hit in four at-bats. The game was tied at 3 through nine innings, but Denver rallied to score four runs in the top of the tenth to win the game, 7-3.

Near the end of March, the Rio Grande League standings showed Wichita in first with a 4-3 record, followed by Des Moines (5-4), Denver (3-4), and Omaha (2-3). Unusually cold weather in the Rio Grande Valley actually forced the postponement of a game between Omaha and Des Moines on March 26. In other training camp notes, the Des Moines team cancelled its plans to play an exhibition game in Northern Mexico, saying that travel time would interfere with the spring training preparations for the team.

A huge crowd in Mission on March 29 watched as Leo Najo's Omaha team pounced on the Denver Bears, 7-2. Batting fourth and playing centerfield, Najo scored twice and had a single in 5 at-bats.

Omaha Packers	AB	R	H	E
Hetherly, 3b	2	0	0	0
Berka, 3b	2	1	1	1
Faber, ss	4	0	1	0
Najo, cf	5	2	1	0
Sperber, rf	5	2	2	1
Taylor, lf	2	0	1	0
Owens, lf	0	1	0	0
Senne, 1b	3	0	1	0
Tierney, 2b	3	0	1	1
King, 2b	2	0	0	0
Carlson, c	3	1	0	0
Tutwiler, p	2	0	1	0
Busby, p	0	0	0	0
Perry, p	1	0	1	0
TOTALS	34	7	10	3

	1	2	3	4	5	6	7	8	9	-	R	H	E
Denver	0	0	0	2	0	0	0	0	0	-	2	5	4
Omaha	2	1	0	1	0	0	4	0	x	-	7	10	3

LEO NAJO: BASEBALL'S FIRST LATINO SUPERSTAR

On March 31, Najo hit a homerun in the first inning of a game against Des Moines. He went on to collect two hits in four at-bats and scored two runs, although Omaha lost 8-13 in a rain-shortened game. On the same day, another high-scoring affair took place between the Wichita Aviators and the Denver Bears, in which eleven homeruns were hit. The teams combined for 39 hits, as Wichita prevailed by the score of 17-11.

On April Fools' Day in Mission, Omaha extracted revenge on Des Moines with a 9-1 victory in which Najo scored three runs. Leo had one hit in one official at-bat.

Omaha moved on to San Benito for an April 2 contest against the Denver Bears. Najo moved to third in the batting order and responded by pounding out two hits and scoring one run. With the game tied 1-1 after nine innings, Najo stroked a single into left field in the tenth inning and later scored, as Omaha pushed across nine runs for a 10-1 victory over Denver.

The Lower Rio Grande Valley League actually took an "all-star break" of sorts on April 4, as the city of Harlingen hosted an exhibition game between the major league Pittsburgh Pirates and an all-star team comprised of Western League players. Only 500 fans showed up at Harlingen's Fair Park to watch the Pirates emerge with a hard-fought 3-2 victory. Mission's Leo Najo did not play in the game.

On April 5 in San Benito, Omaha held a slim 2-1 lead over Denver going into the ninth inning. Najo opened the frame with a walk, and then he advanced to third on a single and a fly ball. A teammate's single brought Najo and another player home. Before the ninth inning ended, Omaha had scored four times to win the game, 6-1. Najo, who batted third and played centerfield, finished with one hit in three at-bats and one run scored.

Omaha and Denver moved their series to Mission for an April 6 contest, in which Najo got two singles in five turns at bat. Six errors and marginal pitching produced a sloppy game that was finally won by Denver, 13-10.

Najo had an outstanding game at the plate on April 8 against Des Moines. He collected three hits, including a double, in four at-bats and scored two runs, propelling Omaha to a 13-12 victory. Scoring:

	1	2	3	4	5	6	7	8	9	-	R	H	E
Omaha	3	0	3	1	1	0	4	0	1	-	13	11	2
Des Moines	5	4	2	1	0	0	0	0	0	-	12	11	3

Omaha Packers	AB	R	H	E
Hetherly, 3b	5	1	1	1
Faber, 2b	5	2	1	1
Najo, cf	4	2	3	0
Spurber, rf	5	1	1	0
Taylor, lf	5	1	2	0
Senne, 1b	3	2	0	0
Tierney, ss	3	1	1	0
Burns, c	3	0	1	0
Anderson, c	1	2	1	0
Shanahan, p	2	0	0	0
Bornholdt, p	2	1	0	0
TOTALS	38	13	11	2

Des Moines	AB	R	H	E
Hughes, cf	5	3	3	0
Nielsen, ss	3	1	1	1
Lowrance, 2b	1	0	0	0
Berger, lf	1	1	1	0
Nebelung, lf	4	1	2	0
Oglesby, 1b	4	1	2	0
Van Camp, rf	3	2	1	0
Windham, 3b	4	1	1	0
Atwell, 2b-ss	3	1	1	1
Sypher, c	5	0	1	0
Tinning, p	1	1	0	0
Birkofer, p	2	0	1	0
Davenport, p	1	0	0	0
TOTALS	37	12	12	3

"The hard, dry field made fielding of ground balls a hazardous job, and balls hit, which could have been fielded went bouncing merrily over the infielder's heads on many occasions," the Harlingen newspaper reported. The scoring for the game was:

As of April 7, Wichita (11-6) was first in the Rio Grande League, followed by Des Moines (8-8), Omaha (7-9), and Denver (7-10).

On April 9, Najo and the Omaha Packers hosted a doubleheader in Mission against the Des Moines Demons. Najo again had a strong performance at the plate, as he pounded out two hits and scored twice in the first game, as Omaha won, 14-11. In the second game, ten Omaha runners crossed the plate in the second inning, which led to a 12-8 victory for Najo's Packers. "All but one of those knocks was pitiful to behold for they were ground balls that took sudden high hops on the hard diamond over the heads of the infielders or were bloopers just out of the reach of infield and outfield," the local paper reported.

On April 10, Des Moines suffered its seventh straight loss, 7-8, at the hands of Wichita. The Rio Grande League standings of April 13 showed Wichita at 15-9, followed by Omaha (13-12), Des Moines (11-14), and Denver (10-14).

On April 11 in San Benito, Najo's Omaha team took a hard-fought win over the Denver Bears, 6-5, with Leo scoring one of his team's runs and collecting one hit in four at-bats. The score by innings was:

	1	2	3	4	5	6	7	8	9	-	R	H	E
Omaha	0	0	0	4	2	0	0	0	0	-	6	8	2
Denver	5	4	2	1	0	0	0	0	0	-	12	11	3

In the final action of the spring training league's 30-game season, doubleheaders were played to cap nearly two months of exciting baseball action. Najo's Omaha Packers beat Wichita 14-2 in the first of two, but they lost the second game, 5-15. Meanwhile, Des Moines and Denver also split their twin bill, with Denver winning 11-4, followed by a Des Moines victory, 4-3.

The Wichita Aviators, who were based in McAllen, won the league "championship". Najo's Omaha team, based in Mission, finished second, followed by Des Moines (Harlingen) and Denver (San Benito).

Harlingen's *Valley Morning Star* summed up the season by saying, "The Valley Western league season has come to a close – no more baseball will be played. The season closed yesterday, doubleheaders sending them on their way to the Western league section where they open the season this weekend. The Western league clubs were in the Valley for a period of almost seven weeks. The Giants, White Sox and Pirates sent rookie clubs down for games, all of which drew well. The Western league games did not draw as well as was expected. Every town lost money."

Thus ended the impromptu Lower Rio Grande Valley League, a temporary offshoot of the Western Association. The teams left the Valley on April 15 to begin preparations for the start of the regular season on April 19.

Chapter 12
Omaha, Year Two (1930)

Before the start of Najo's second year in Omaha in 1930, the new manager, Spencer Abbott told *The Sporting News* that he expected his squad to have "punch," referring to hitting power. "I am a firm believer in punch on a ball club. Every winner in baseball must have a wrecking crew... Riley, Taylor, Sperber, and Najo will be ours, and then we'll have Kettle Wirts down there near the end of the lineup to shake up things."

An interesting development in 1930 was the coming of night baseball to the Western League. Before the season started, the Des Moines Demons announced that lights were being installed at their stadium. According to the *Encyclopedia of Minor League Baseball*, when Des Moines played a night game on May 2, it was the first game in the history of Organized Baseball to be played under permanent light standards. "Many scoffed at the idea, but owner Lee Keyser had installed a high-quality system. The results were immediate. Play was not adversely affected, and fans came out in large numbers." Previously, only a few night baseball games had been played using portable lighting.

Night baseball is credited with keeping the minor leagues afloat during the horrendous period of nationwide economic turmoil from 1929 to 1941. This technological innovation, more than any other factor, allowed the game to remain economically feasible in the wake of the Great Depression. By the end of the decade, according to author Robert Obojski, "night games became so popular throughout the minors – and so very profitable to the club owners – that the majority of weekday games were played under the arc lights."

The Western League's other teams expressed a high degree of interest in the Des Moines experiment. Many people immediately saw the potential of night baseball to increase attendance and league revenues. Shortly after the season started, Omaha also began installing lights at its ballpark.

The Omaha team, which changed its name from Crickets to Packers before the season started, was not expected to do well in the 1930 Western League race. An April 24 article in *The Sporting News* noted that the team's pitching was suspect, although its hitting and fielding were expected to be top notch. "Leo Najo is a fixture in center field" said an article by sportswriter Harold George.

On opening day, Saturday April 19, against the Oklahoma City Indians, Najo connected on three hits, including a double, in four at-bats, as Omaha won 9-5. On the following day, Oklahoma City stormed back and won both ends of a doubleheader. But on April 21, Najo went 2-for-2 and made seven outfield putouts in leading his team to a 4-1 win over the Indians, and on the following day, he went 3-for-4 and stole a base in a 14-9 win over Wichita. Najo's base hit and five putouts also lead to a dramatic 5-4 victory over Wichita on April 24.

In another fantastic game on May 3 at Topeka, Kansas, Najo hit two doubles and made eight outfield putouts in a 10-6 win. He continued to pile on the multi-hit games and the doubles through the rest of May, in addition to playing stellar defense. He collected two singles versus Denver on May 5, a double against Wichita on May 8, and two singles against Oklahoma City on May 11.

As the early season progressed, technicians in Omaha were busy installing lights at the ballpark. On May 15, *The Sporting News* reported, "The lighting equipment for the Omaha park is being installed by the Giant Manufacturing Company of Council Bluffs, Iowa, a concern which has specialized in lighting plants for outdoor night events. It has been announced that the Packer Park will be ready for nocturnal baseball within a short time." The article also mentioned that not all team owners in the Western League supported night baseball and that one of them commented, "People are not going to stay up until 11 or 12 o'clock to watch ball games."

Like many of the ballplayers of his era, Najo was not thrilled at the idea of night baseball. Until stadium illumination became much more sophisticated, not to mention brighter, many years later, playing baseball in shadowy semi-darkness was not a pleasant thought for most players, except maybe for pitchers. For fielders, the errors were sure to pile up and the risk of injury was sure to increase. Nonetheless, from a marketing perspective, night baseball was a no-brainer, because spectators could attend games after their workday ended, instead of having to take time off from work.

Najo in Omaha, 1930 (Courtesy of Athit Farias)

Omaha maintained a .500 winning percentage in May, and Najo continued hitting the ball very well, following up on the success of his 41 doubles in 1929. Through May 15, Najo's amazing batting average of .408 ranked him second in the league in hitting. On May 13, Najo hit a triple and a homerun in a 13-10 triumph over the Western League's newest team, the St. Joseph Saints, an affiliate of the St. Louis Cardinals. Najo followed up the performance with another homerun on the next day to give his team a 5-4 win over the Saints.

On the St. Joseph pitching staff was a youngster named Jay Hanna "Dizzy" Dean. The future major league Hall of Fame star finished the 1930 season with a 17-8 record (.632) in 217 innings pitched. Before

1930 ended, Dizzy Dean was pitching for the major league St. Louis Cardinals.

On May 16, the Omaha Packers stole a total of ten bases, including two by Leo Najo, en route to a 10-7 victory over Des Moines. Najo's three singles on May 23 helped Omaha defeat Pueblo, 6-2, and he added a homerun in the following day's game. As of May 27, Najo's batting average was up to .414, and he was just one percentage point behind the league leader.

Riding the strength of Najo's hitting and defense, the Omaha Packers attained first place in the Western League on June 3, with a 22-16 (.578) record. At Denver on May 19, Najo hit a triple and a single. *The Sporting News* reported, "Najo of Omaha staged a hitting spurt last week to take the lead over the other Western League hitters. He had a mark of .425."

On Thursday May 29, Najo and the Packers played their first night game at home. About 7,000 fans showed up at Omaha's Vinton Street Park to usher in the era of night baseball. The Denver Bears, behind the strong pitching of Ed Greer, limited the home team to just four hits, including one by Leo Najo. Although Omaha lost 0-4, the lights were a hit with the spectators, and by the end of the season, all but two of the teams in the Western League made the transition to lighted ballparks.

A double and a stolen base by Najo led to an 8-3 Omaha win over Pueblo on June 1. He hit yet another homerun on June 5 against Oklahoma City. In a doubleheader against Wichita on June 8, Najo had a double, a single, and a stolen base in the first game, and he hit a homerun in the nightcap. Omaha won both games.

Najo continued his hot hitting in June, as noted in a *Sporting News* article: "Najo of Omaha with an average of .379 was the nominal batting monarch of the Western League for games up to June 16." At the same time that Najo claimed the batting lead, his team remained in first place in the league with a 34-24 record (.586). "President Barney Burch of the Omaha Packers is wearing one of those smiles that are hard to rub off these days. Night baseball and a winning team have packed the fans into the Packer Park, after Burch had been drifting along with indifferent support for several year," said *The Sporting News*.

LEO NAJO: BASEBALL'S FIRST LATINO SUPERSTAR

On June 16, in a 13-9 victory over Topeka, Najo hit a homerun and a single. He then hit a series of doubles over the course of several games late in June. Najo's team, with a 40-28 record (.588) on July 1, remained first in the league, although the Wichita Aviators were a very close second at 40-31 (.563).

On June 22 against St. Joseph, Najo went 2-for-2 at the plate and had two stolen bases to lead Omaha to a 6-5 win. One day later, he hit a double and two singles in an 8-4 Omaha victory. A double and a stolen base by Najo on June 26 led to yet another win, this time 13-5 over Topeka.

By the end of June, night baseball was spreading throughout the league, even among teams who had previously opposed it. The success of the teams that had already installed lights, including Omaha, caused the other owners to reconsider their previous objections.

On July 17, Najo's hot streak at the plate had cooled a bit, and his batting average began dropping. After 84 games, Najo had 112 hits and 62 runs in 319 at-bats with 68 runs-batted-in and a .361 batting average. He ranked eighth among league batting leaders as of July 17, although his team remained in the league's top position, with a 58-40 record on July 29.

As the month of August began, the Wichita Aviators slipped ahead of Omaha in the race for the league title. Najo's hitting picked up, as he slammed a homerun on July 28, a double and a single on July 29, a single on August 1, and a single and stolen base on August 2.

Through August 1, Najo had appeared in 100 games with 378 at-bats, 127 hits, 76 runs, 80 runs-batted-in, and a .336 average. He unleashed a series of doubles during August, though he did not have as many multi-hit games as he did earlier in the season. On August 20, his batting average was .340 with 148 hits in 435 at-bats.

On August 27, Najo played in a night game at Omaha against the Denver Bears. He had a single in four plate appearances and made three outfield assists, but his team lost 4-6. It was to be Najo's last game of the season, as the league suddenly suspended him for "rule violations," the nature of which were not specified by league officials.

Although the exact reason for Najo's suspension remains unknown, an article in *The Sporting News* following the incident stated that he was suspended "near the end of the season for playing against a team that harbored several ineligible players." No further explanation was given.

The league's final statistics showed that Leo Najo had appeared in 129 of the team's 142 games, and he had 471 at-bats, 168 hits, 98 runs, 92 runs-batted-in, 77 bases on balls, and a .335 final average (11th in the league). Of his 168 hits, he had 41 doubles, 8 triples, and 6 homeruns. Defensively, Najo made 341 outfield putouts in 129 games, with 10 assists and only 9 errors, for a fielding percentage of .975 (4th in the league among outfielders).

When the season ended on September 2, the final standings were:

Team	*W*	*L*	*Pct*	*GB*
Wichita Aviators	89	56	.614	--
Omaha Packers	76	66	.535	11 ½
Oklahoma City Indians	79	71	.527	12 ½
Des Moines Demons	77	71	.520	13 ½
Pueblo Braves	75	75	.500	16 ½
Denver Bears	74	74	.500	16 ½
Topeka Senators	66	84	.440	25 ½
St. Joseph Saints	53	92	.366	36

Najo had completed another highly successful season in the Western League, having finished with the highest batting average on his team, along with his other accomplishments. With Najo's talents on display, Omaha almost captured the league title, falling just 11 ½ games short. Amazingly, despite his excellent play, Najo was not selected to the league's all-star team, which may have been a result of the prevailing racial prejudice of the time.

Chapter 13
Omaha to San Antonio (1931)

Minor league baseball's economic woes continued in 1931, despite the growing popularity of night games. Although 24 minor leagues started the 1931 season, only 16 would finish it. Unfortunately, as Leo Najo's career peaked, allowing him to finally seek a good salary, the Great Depression intervened, severely hampering the ability of the minor leagues to pay their players a fair wage.

Heading into the 1931 season, Omaha owner Barney Burch faced significant challenges with his team. First, the team's manager, Spencer Abbott, left to go manage the Portland Beavers of the Class AA Pacific Coast League. Burch quickly brought in Herb "Doc" Smith to replace him. Second, Burch was dissatisfied with the old ballpark that his team had been using, as it had deteriorated badly during the 1930 season, and he had elected not to renew his lease on it. He toyed with the idea of building a new ballpark. Third, from his 1930 team that finished second in the league, only five players were returning for 1931, including center fielder Leo Najo. Burch faced the prospect of having to build virtually a new team with a new manager and possibly a new ballpark.

Despite these obstacles, Burch told *The Sporting News* that he looked forward to the 1931 season, "Night baseball netted me a nice profit, and I think we'll have another good year this season." Indeed, night baseball was no longer a fad, and many of the 1931 games were played under lights.

Burch made another change in 1931, and most other league owners followed suit. He decided that, due to the mild spring forecast for Nebraska, he would hold spring training at home, instead of traveling south as in previous years.

As preparations for the new season began, Leo Najo was projected to again be the team's starter at centerfield. "Leo Najo, who batted .335 last year as a Packer, is a cinch for center field," said *The*

Sporting News. In addition, Najo's team was picked to finish no higher than fourth in the league.

On opening day, Thursday, April 30, at St. Joseph, Missouri, Leo Najo hit a double, a single, and stole a base, as Omaha defeated the Saints 5-2. The following day, Najo had two singles in four trips to the plate, and he made six outfield putouts, as Omaha won again, 11-4. Najo's stolen base and three putouts also helped win the third game of the opening series, 5-2.

While Omaha struggled to a 5-6 record, the defending champion Wichita Aviators reeled off eleven wins in a row to start the season. Wichita beat Omaha 4-1 on May 3, despite a double, a single, and four putouts by Najo. On May 4, Najo hit a double in a 9-11 loss to Wichita, followed by a single the next day in a 2-4 loss.

Najo's triple and single on May 9 helped Omaha defeat Oklahoma City, 6-0. He continued to play well through the next two weeks, and on May 19, he went 2-for-3 with a double in a 4-2 win over Topeka. Against Wichita on May 24, Leo went 3-for-4, but Omaha lost the game, 8-11. In Denver on May 31, Najo had three hits, including a homerun, only to see his team lose to the Bears, 13-14.

Although Najo performed at a consistently good level in 1931, the Omaha team as a whole did very poorly. By June 9, the Packers found themselves in last place, with a 13-21 record (.382). The team's owner began adding and subtracting players in an effort to induce some victories.

On Sunday, June 7, Najo hit a double and made five putouts in the first game of a doubleheader against Des Moines, which Omaha won 5-3. Then he hit a single, a double, and a triple for a 14-11 win in the nightcap. In another doubleheader on June 12, Najo hit two doubles to give Omaha a 3-2 win in the first game and then went 3-for-3 in a 5-4 second game victory. Despite Najo's efforts, the team continued to slump, and on June 11, manager Doc Smith resigned, telling *The Sporting News*, "Something is wrong with the team and I can't find out what it is. It must be me. So I was willing to quit to give the team a chance to find out." The team's owner, Barney Burch, temporarily took over as manager, and about a month later, veteran first baseman Francis "Pug" Griffin was named manager.

LEO NAJO: BASEBALL'S FIRST LATINO SUPERSTAR

In a June 14 game against Denver, Najo hit two singles and stole a base as Omaha beat the Bears, 5-4. On the 16th in an 8-5 win over Oklahoma City, Najo went 3-for-4 with two doubles. Leo continued to be productive through the rest of May, both on offense and defense; however, his batting average was nowhere near what it had been in 1930. There were occasional flashes of Najo's previous form, such as in a June 28 doubleheader against Wichita, when he had six hits, including a double and a triple.

Najo, Circa. 1930s (Courtesy of Alicia Farias)

When the first half of the season ended on July 10, Omaha stood at 29-38 and in seventh place in the league.

After falling out of the lineup on June 30, Najo returned to action on July 3 but went hitless against Des Moines. Versus Denver on July 8, Najo went 3-for-5 with a double in a 7-5 win, and two days later, he went 3-for-3 with a double in a loss to Denver. Najo's hitting picked up steam during the last two weeks of July, as he went 3-for-4 on July 14, 3-for-4 on July 17, and 2-for-4 on July 18. The hitting spurt moved Najo into third place in the league batting statistics. As of July 21, through 74 games, Najo had 95 hits in 262 at-bats with 63 runs and one homerun. His batting average stood at .363.

With a 5-14 start in the second half of the season, Omaha immediately occupied last place in the league, where they remained for the rest of the season. Though Najo continued to hit doubles and have multi-hit games, his team kept losing. Occasionally when Najo was really hot, Omaha did manage to win, such as on August 7, when Najo's two doubles led to an 8-6 victory over Topeka.

Through August 11, Najo's batting average was .356, and in 92 games, he had collected 119 hits in 334 at-bats, with 78 runs. These were to be his final Western League statistics because, despite his good numbers (or maybe because of them), he was traded away. The move was undoubtedly prompted by the team's need to generate money.

With only about a month remaining in the season, Omaha traded Najo to San Antonio of the Texas League in exchange for outfielder Monk Edwards. Like Omaha, San Antonio was mired in last place in their league at the time of the trade. A San Antonio sportswriter said, "'Najo as a fielder has always been unbeatable and he has greatly improved in batting during the time he has been with Barney Burch's Omaha Packers in the Western League, the recent averages showing his mark at .353 and besides Najo is lightning fast on the bases. Najo has been taken in trade for Monk Edwards for the reason that he is a better fielder. Najo is the best on shoestring catches of any player that has ever been seen on the local lot, and this includes major as well as minor leaguers, for Leonardo Alaniz, which is Najo's real name, is the headliner in this specialty."

After driving his car from Omaha straight to San Antonio, Najo joined the Indians on August 11 for a game against Beaumont. Playing left field for the San Antonio, Najo was 1-for-3 at the plate and made three outfield putouts in a 0-5 loss. Describing the putouts, the *San Antonio Express* said, '"Najo leaped into the spotlight on a long running catch of White's fly near the left center fence and then dashed in on the next play to take Hughes' pop fly back of third base. Najo killed a base hit for Taylor in the eighth as he ran in to dip the ball with his gloved hand just above his shoe tops."

One night later, Najo hit a single in a 2-3 loss to Galveston. On August 13, he moved back into centerfield. In a doubleheader against Wichita Falls on August 14, Leo went 2-for-3 in the first game and 1-for-2 in the second, both losses. Najo's single and stolen base on August 15 helped San Antonio win 5-3 in the opening game of a doubleheader, and his single in the second game contributed to an 8-3 win.

In a doubleheader against Fort Worth on August 16, Najo went 2-for-3 and lead the Indians to a 5-3 victory in the first game and then collected two more hits in the second game, which was a 2-4 loss. Another two-hit performance on August 24 helped beat Dallas 7-6. A double and a homerun on August 27, however, could not prevent a San Antonio loss to Shreveport, 6-7.

In a 7-3 win over Dallas on August 30, Najo hit a double and a single, and he made seven outfield putouts.

When the second half of the Texas League season ended on September 13, Najo's team finished in last place with a 31-50 (.383) record. Though Najo played well, San Antonio's season was already beyond salvaging by the time Najo arrived from Omaha. The final standings for both of the leagues in which Najo played in 1931 were:

Team (Western League)	*W*	*L*	*Pct*	*GB*
Des Moines Demons	94	51	.648	--
Wichita Aviators	92	58	.613	4 ½
St. Joseph Saints	79	64	.552	14
Pueblo Braves	76	69	.524	18
Oklahoma City Indians	70	80	.467	16 ½
Denver Bears	64	77	.454	28
Topeka Senators	58	86	.397	35 ½
Omaha Packers	49	97	.336	45 ½

Team (Texas League)	W	L	Pct	GB
Houston Buffaloes	108	51	.679	--
Beaumont Exporters	94	65	.591	14
Ft. Worth Panthers	90	70	.563	18 ½
Dallas Steers	83	77	.519	25 ½
Wichita Falls Spudders	76	85	.472	33
Shreveport Sports	66	94	.413	42 ½
San Antonio Indians	66	94	.413	42 ½
Galveston Buccaneers	57	104	.354	52

In 39 games with San Antonio, Najo batted 124 times and had 32 hits, scored 17 runs, sacrificed 25 times, stole 15 bases, and had a .266 batting average. Defensively, in 24 games at left field, Najo had 48 putouts without an error and ranked second in the league among left fielders. In 15 games at centerfield, he had 34 putouts with no error, ranking him fourth among the league's center fielders.

Chapter 14
San Antonio to Tulsa (1932)

In addition to the country's continuing economic problems, declining attendance also plagued both the Texas and Western leagues. San Antonio's attendance fell from 106,517 in 1928 to 31,761 in 1932. Because of sagging attendance and other financial pressures, the minor leagues cut player salaries sharply during 1932 and 1933. According to the operating guidelines of the National Association adopted for 1933, the monthly salary limit for each team in class A was set at $4,250 for 16 players, exclusive of the manager (unless the manager also played). This means that the maximum average salary per player was $265 per month. In addition, many leagues set a maximum salary per player of $250. Given the financial difficulties of the time, however, the monthly salary for most players and teams was well below the limit, and many players received closer to $150 per month.

Before the start of the 1932 season, the Texas League reduced both the maximum number of players a team could have on its roster and the maximum salary that teams could pay their players. An article in *The Sporting News* explained, "In line with economic conditions over the country, the league put into effect drastic economies for 1932. The player limit, raised in 1927 to 18 men, was reduced to 17... In addition, the league adopted an individual salary limit and a club salary limit well below the figures of the past four years and put teeth in the salary limit enforcement legislation."

The article continued, "The economies were made necessary, it was pointed out, because of heavy losses experienced by individual clubs over a period of years, which were aggravated by general economic conditions in 1931."

Leo Najo started the financially troubled 1932 season in San Antonio, but he was destined to spend most of the season playing in Tulsa, Oklahoma. Tulsa had a team in the Western League from 1919 to 1929, but after winning the league championship in 1929, the team abandoned the city. Early in 1932, rumors began to circulate that the

Wichita Aviators were moving to Tulsa. A February 4 *Sporting News* article said, "The Wichita franchise in the Western League is to be transferred to Tulsa, Okla., according to Art Griggs, manager.... The Pittsburgh Pirates, who maintain a working agreement with Wichita, are said to have sanctioned the move."

The Wichita Aviators won the Western League title in 1930 and finished second in 1931. With the core of the Wichita team transferring to Oklahoma, the expectations of Tulsa fans were running high as preparations began for the new season. The Tulsa Oilers were projected to finish third, behind Des Moines and Denver, in preseason predictions.

Back in San Antonio, Leo Najo, now 33 years old, had no idea that his path would soon intersect with that of the Tulsa Oilers. With baseball season about to begin, Najo was still in San Antonio, playing for the Indians of the Texas League. In an interesting twist for Najo, the major league team that once drafted him, the Chicago White Sox, held their 1932 spring training in San Antonio, and Leo got a chance to face them in exhibition play.

First-year White Sox manager Lew Fonsaca and his team opened camp in San Antonio on March 3 with an afternoon of light drills. Credited with pioneering the use of film to improve player performance, Fonsaca began using film at around this time. His 1932 team was not one of Chicago's strongest, but it did include several outstanding players, such as Ted Lyons and spitball wizard Red Faber, both of whom had been on the 1926 team with Najo.

The White Sox originally planned to use school district facilities for their spring camp but found them unacceptable. The team made hasty negotiations with the Texas League to use League Park instead, and the San Antonio Indians reluctantly agreed to allow it. The agreed-upon schedule required that the Indians finish their training each day by 1 p.m., after which the White Sox would take over the ballpark.

Due to unseasonably cold weather, both teams spent a lot of time practicing indoor early in March. Chicago owner J. Louis Comisky expressed to the media his displeasure that "sunny Texas" turned out to be otherwise. But on March 19, the San Antonio Indians and the

LEO NAJO: BASEBALL'S FIRST LATINO SUPERSTAR

White Sox finally had their day in the sun, hooking up in their first exhibition match. The game resulted in a 16-2 Chicago victory.

On the following day, Chicago took an 8-4 win, a game in which Najo did not participate. Leo did finally get to face his old team on March 23. In their final exhibition game in San Antonio, the White Sox used future Hall of Famer Ted Lyons as their starting pitcher. Najo, who played left field, saw limited action in the game, recording only one putout and failing to get a hit in only one at-bat. The White Sox defeated the Indians, 13-5, after which the Chicagoans packed their bags and left town. With the White Sox gone, Najo and the Indians focused their attention on the start of the Texas League season.

Opening day was Wednesday, April 13, as Najo and the San Antonio Indians traveled to Beaumont for a game against the Exporters. Najo, playing in right field and batting leadoff, picked up where he left off in 1931, collecting three hits in four plate appearances, but San Antonio still lost, 11-1. One day later, Najo hit a single and stole a base, as the Indians lost again. In the third game of the season, a loss to Houston, Najo hit a double and a single.

On April 18, Najo had two singles in a 6-4 win over Galveston. On April 20, he had a triple and two singles in a 9-6 victory. A triple and a single led to a 4-0 win over Galveston on April 21. Two days later in Houston, Najo went 3-for-4, as the Indians won, 7-3. With a 9-9 start on the new season, San Antonio seemed on its way, and Najo appeared to be an integral part of their success.

On May 4, Najo went 3-for-4 in a 3-1 win over Dallas. A double and a stolen base from Leo helped San Antonio beat Shreveport 4-3 on May 12. Najo appeared as a pinch hitter on May 16 in a 0-3 loss to Dallas and again on May 20 in a 4-5 loss to Fort Worth. After that, he was benched and did not appear in any more games for San Antonio. Evidence suggests that team owners were shopping him around to other teams.

As fate would have it, by leaving the team in May, Najo missed the excitement of watching the team's home stadium, League Park, burn to the ground on the evening of June 18, 1932. Following a game between the Indians and the Dallas Steers, a fire broke out in the wooden bleachers. In his book *San Antonio at Bat*, author David King writes, "Three minutes after the fire was reported, it had spread throughout the wooden grandstands, which were topped with a freshly tarred roof. At the fire's height, flames and smoke could be seen for miles."

Najo's final statistics for San Antonio showed that in 33 games, he had 129 at-bats, with 31 hits, a .250 batting average, 19 runs, 8 runs-batted-in, 14 bases on balls, and 3 stolen bases. His 31 hits included six doubles, two triples, and no homeruns. Defensively, Najo played right field in 30 games and had 33 putouts without an error. At the end of the 1932 Texas League season, despite his limited playing time, he ranked third in fielding among all right fielders.

Back in Tulsa, during the first week of May, the Oilers' starting center fielder, Leo Nonnenkamp, fractured his ankle while sliding into a base, and Tulsa began looking for a replacement. Nonnenkamp, a rookie, had been hitting .416 at the time of his injury. Tulsa manager Art Griggs tried several different players at the position but soon realized that his team needed an experienced player in order to maintain the club's position at the top of the league standings.

Late in May, Griggs contacted San Antonio and obtained the services of Leo Najo. On June 2, *The Sporting News* reported, "Leo Najo, little Mexican outfielder, has been released outright by the San Antonio Indians to Tulsa of the Western League."

Najo joined his new team on Wednesday, May 25 for a night game against the St. Joseph Saints. He started at centerfield and batted sixth in the lineup. In a 5-3 victory for Tulsa, Najo had a single and five outfield putouts.

In his second game for Tulsa, Najo moved up to fifth in the lineup and went 3-for-4 in a 2-0 victory over the Oklahoma City Indians. In a doubleheader on May 29, Tulsa drilled the Indians 11-4 and 11-1, as Najo collected one hit in each game and one stolen base, plus a total of six putouts. The acquisition of Najo was beginning to pay dividends for the league-leading Tulsa Oilers.

On May 30, Najo went 3-for-5 with a double and had eight putouts in the first game of another doubleheader against Oklahoma City, and then he went 3-for-5 with a homerun and a double in the nightcap.

Whereas San Antonio appeared to be going nowhere and had benched him before his release, Najo suddenly found himself on one of the best teams in baseball. Through June 6, Tulsa stood at 28-17 (.622) and held first place in the league, followed closely by Des Moines (25-15), Omaha (26-21), and Wichita (24-22).

The Oilers then reeled off a string of victories, during which Najo was in top form on both offense and defense. On June 5, in a doubleheader against Pueblo, Najo went 2-for-4 in the first game and then hit a double in the second game, which Tulsa won, 18-10.

Najo continued to have success at the plate, and Tulsa kept winning its games. On June 8, his 3-for-4 performance helped Tulsa beat Omaha, 8-5. By the middle of June, Tulsa had a 40-20 (.687) record and started to put some distance between itself and the other teams.

While he was not showing tremendous power, Najo was hitting singles consistently, driving in runs, drawing walks, and catching everything that came his way in the outfield. Tulsa could not have asked for anything more, as the team made its run for the Western League championship. On June 18, Najo went 2-for-4 to lead Tulsa to a 12-10 victory over Pueblo. On June 27, he was 2-for-3 in a 7-4 win over Omaha. A pair of doubles, two singles, and four putouts on June 28 helped win both ends of a doubleheader against Omaha by scores of 8-2 and 12-6.

With Najo a fixture at centerfield, Tulsa moved confidently into July, still leading the league and scoring a series of impressive victories. When the first half of the season ended on June 30, the league standings showed:

Team	W	L	Pct
Tulsa Oilers	46	22	.676
Denver Bears	42	32	.568
Des Moines Demons	36	30	.545
Omaha Packers	36	37	.493
St. Joseph Saints	33	36	.493
Wichita Aviators	33	37	.471
Oklahoma City Indians	31	41	.431
Pueblo Braves	25	49	.338

On July 3, Najo hit a double to help Tulsa edge Oklahoma City, 4-3. On the Fourth of July, Najo contributed a triple to Tulsa's 10-0 win over the Indians, and he hit another triple on the following day against the same team.

In a tremendously exciting game on Friday, July 8, Tulsa trailed St. Joseph 9-11 in the bottom of the ninth, when the Oilers exploded for three runs and won the game 12-11. Leo Najo went 2-for-4 at the plate and stole a base. On July 10, Najo got a two-base hit and five outfield putouts in leading his team to a 4-3 triumph over St. Joseph. Two days later, Najo's triple helped Tulsa beat Wichita, 8-3. He then went 2-for-4 with three putouts in downing Wichita, 9-7, on July 13. Wichita fell once again on July 14, thanks to Najo's 2-for-3 performance at the plate.

Najo's hitting continued to improve after the season's halfway point, while he remained rock steady in fielding his position. On July 17-20, Najo put together an outstanding series of at-bats against Tulsa and St. Joseph, going 3-for-5, 3-for-4, 2-for-5, and 3-for-5.

Leo had a great game against Pueblo on July 31, in which he hit a homerun and a double, en route to an 11-1 win. On August 3, in a very exciting game, Najo went 2-for-2 with a double to help defeat Tulsa, 5-4. With only about a month left in the second half of the season, Najo's team stood at 34-17 and in second place behind Oklahoma City (35-17). By August 23, the Oilers were in first place at 41-10.

On August 7, Najo was 3-for-3 with a double and four outfield putouts in a 7-5 win over Denver. He followed that performance up with a couple of 2-for-5 games against Pueblo. On August 17, Najo hit a homerun and two singles to beat Des Moines, 6-5. Two days later, he went 2-for-4 and led his team to a 7-3 win over Wichita.

In the last three weeks of the season, Najo intensified his hitting, reeling off numerous multi-hit games. A double and a single against Wichita on August 29 led to a 2-0 win. On August 31, he went 2-for-5 in a 10-5 win over St. Joseph and then 3-for-4 with two doubles on the following night in an 8-3 victory over Oklahoma City.

In a dramatic finish to the season, Oklahoma City defeated Tulsa four times in the last week of play to finish with a won-loss record for the second half (52-26) that was identical to that of Tulsa. This forced a best-of-three playoff for the second-half title.

Najo Leaps for a Fly Ball (Courtesy of Alicia Farias)

The playoff became a necessity only after Oklahoma City defeated Tulsa 7-3 in the final regular season game on September 7.

A crowd of 8,000 watched in Oklahoma City's home park, as the Indians' last-gasp effort to make the playoffs succeeded.

In the resulting best-of-three playoff, if Tulsa won, the Oilers were automatically the winners of the pennant. If Oklahoma City won the playoff, they would force a best-of-seven league championship series against Tulsa. So, in effect, in order to win the league pennant, Oklahoma City had to beat Tulsa six times.

The playoff series began on September 8 in Oklahoma City with a 5-2 win by the upstart Indians. Najo had a triple in four plate appearances and three outfield putouts. In game two, also in Oklahoma City, Leo Najo drove in the winning run on a sacrifice fly to right field in the tenth inning. Tulsa won 7-6 to even the playoff series at one game apiece. Najo also hit a double in the game.

In the deciding game, which was played in Tulsa, Najo went hitless in four trips to the plate, as Oklahoma City beat the Oilers, 2-1. This set the stage for Najo's team to enter a best-of-seven championship series against the same Oklahoma City team.

The pennant series opened in Tulsa on Sunday, September 11 with a 12-inning affair, in which the winning run for Tulsa scored on a bases-loaded walk in the bottom of the twelfth. Tulsa won 2-1, though Najo did not have a hit in five at-bats.

The second game, also in Tulsa, was equally dramatic, as Najo went 2-for-4 with a double to lead his team to a 6-4 victory. Tulsa led the championship series, 2 games to none.

At Oklahoma City on September 13, Najo had a single in three at-bats and had three outfield putouts, as Tulsa took the third game of the series, 3-0. One more win would give the Oilers the title.

The fourth game was also played in Oklahoma City, and its outcome was in doubt until the final at-bat of the game. With the game tied 5-5 and two Tulsa runners on base, Leo Najo came up to bat in the top of the tenth inning. He had failed to get a hit in four previous trips to the plate, but this time, he blasted a triple that scored two runs and gave Tulsa a 7-5 win and the league pennant.

At season's end, Leo Najo had appeared in 113 games for Tulsa and had 427 at-bats. He produced 138 hits, 81 runs, 94 runs-batted-in, and a batting average of .323, which ranked him 13th among the league's leading hitters. Of his 138 hits, he had 23 doubles, 10 triples, and 3 homeruns. He also stole six bases.

The final regular season league standings were:

Team	W	L	Pct	GB
Tulsa Oilers	98	48	.671	--
Denver Bears	83	64	.565	15 ½
Oklahoma City Indians	83	67	.553	17
Des Moines Demons	71	72	.497	25 ½
St. Joseph Saints	72	75	.490	26 ½
Wichita Aviators	63	86	.423	36 ½
Pueblo Bears	62	90	.408	39
Omaha Packers	58	88	.397	40

In 2001, as part of the 100th anniversary of the minor leagues, baseball historians Bill Weiss and Marshall Wright created a list of the 100 best teams in the history of minor league baseball. Ranked 83rd on their list were the 1932 Tulsa Oilers, about whom they said, "The 1932 Tulsa Oilers were a one-season wonder, entering and exiting the Western League in a short few months. However, despite their brief stay, the team left a lasting legacy, finishing with the top winning percentage in league history."

Weiss and Wright also noted the contributions to Tulsa's success made by Leo Najo: "Center fielder Leo Najo, who hit .323, was one of the first Mexican players in Organized Baseball. Najo, a native of La Lajilla, Nuevo Leon, had a career average of .321 in 1,318 games, mostly with San Antonio and Omaha."

Chapter 15
Fall from Grace and Return to South Texas (1933)

On February 23, 1933, *The Sporting News* reported that a contract was "in the mail" from the Tulsa Oilers to Leo Najo. On March 6, *The Washington Post* said that three former Texas League players on the Tulsa roster, including Leo Najo, would be "going home," in a manner of speaking, because of the Tulsa team's move from the Western League into the Texas League. The article noted that the three Tulsa players "formerly performed in the Lone Star circuit, Najo as a popular hero of San Antonio fans."

Then on March 23, a *Sporting News* article reported the following: "Leo Najo, Texas' most famous Mexican player, after a salary altercation with the Tulsa Oilers, has been given his unconditional release. It is probable that he will retire from Organized Ball, playing semi-pro around Mission, Tex., where he owns a business building and has other real estate."

Even though Najo had proven himself to be one of the nation's top minor league players, team owners, suffering the effects of the nation's deep economic depression, simply could not pay him what he was worth. The shrinking minor league salaries no doubt were felt most intensely by the few minority ball players. Although it is not clear how Najo's salaries stacked up against those of Anglo teammates, baseball historians would most likely agree that he was paid considerably less.

It is not clear how much of the decision to leave the minors was Najo's own. Clearly, the prevailing doom and gloom of the Great Depression was a key factor. Additionally, he was fed up with the travel, with being constantly pressured to perform, with being sold or traded at a moment's whim by owners, with being constantly overlooked and underappreciated, and with being so far away from his family and his roots.

LEO NAJO: BASEBALL'S FIRST LATINO SUPERSTAR

By the spring of 1933, Najo, who was now 34 years old, had played nine seasons in the minor leagues and was tired of the grind. Data collected by the Mission Historical Museum suggests that by 1933 he was psychologically ready to leave the minors. He had toiled hard, accomplished much, and had fallen just one step short of making it in the major leagues. Circumstances had conspired to block him from what would have most likely been a stellar major league career, had not fate intervened. In 1933, Najo had arrived at time for soul searching and for deciding how he was going to spend the rest of his life.

After his release by the Tulsa Oilers, he headed back home to Mission, Texas, to his wife and other family members. He reacquainted himself with old friends and kept himself in playing shape by returning to the semi-pro team that he helped create, the Mission 30-30s. Leaving the hard life of minor league baseball behind him, he focused on helping his family survive the country's hard economic times. He ran his family's tavern, managed his rental properties in Mission, and, as time allowed, played ball just for fun with friends.

Najo's Tavern in Mission (Photo by Noe Torres)

From 1933 to 1937, Najo made the transition from being a player to being a manager, as he spent more time managing and coaching the young players on the Mission 30-30s. Although he still had more playing years ahead of him, Najo's focus began to change more toward managing during this time.

To the people of South Texas, Najo was a living legend. He had made it big and was accorded celebrity status. He had worn the uniform of the Chicago White Sox and had been on some of the best minor league baseball teams in the country. Anytime Leo took the field with the Mission 30-30s, he drew large crowds of enthusiastic fans. To the Latino community of the Rio Grande Valley, he was a symbol of achievement in a society that so often mistreated minorities.

Because of Najo's achievements, the door opened for other Latino professional baseball players in the years that followed. Ironically, in the same year that Najo left pro baseball, Baldomero Melo "Mel" Almada became the first Mexican player to make it as a full-time player on a major league team. In 1933, he hit .341 in 14 games for the Boston Red Sox. He went on to a 9-year career with the Red Sox, Senators, Browns, and Dodgers.

Najo had come very close to making it in the majors in 1925, eight full years before Almada. Najo may have had another chance at it in 1926, had he not broken his leg playing for San Antonio. Despite the adverse circumstances, Najo simply continued playing his heart out on the field, forcing himself to become one of the greatest minor league players of his time.

Although he still had a few more years of professional baseball ahead of him, for the most part, after 1933, he focused most of his time and energy on being a player, manager, coach, and umpire for the Valley's semi-pro and youth circuits.

For a four-year span, from 1933 to 1937, Najo played and managed the Mission 30-30s and tended to family and business matters. It certainly must have been gratifying for him, after nine grueling years of traveling on buses and trains to play in remote areas of the country, to just stay close to home in his beloved city of Mission. He seemed to have little intention of heading back out on the road to try to make it in professional baseball again, as he settled into

LEO NAJO: BASEBALL'S FIRST LATINO SUPERSTAR

a comfortable routine of playing and managing "just for fun" with the 30-30s.

Chapter 16
The Mission 30-30s (1933-1937)

Today, only an empty field of tall weeds and scrawny mesquite trees remains in Mission, where the mighty "30-30 Rifles" semi-pro team enjoyed some of its finest seasons. Located northeast of the intersection of Walsh Avenue and Perez Street, the field was once the site of the 30-30 stadium, an impressive baseball field boasting covered wooden bleachers from third base around to first. Walking quietly across the hard ground where the stadium once stood, with a gentle southeasterly breeze rustling the abundant foxtails, one can almost hear the voices of the past chanting "Najo! Najo!" It is breathtaking to imagine the faces of the many fans who filled these stands over the years and who witnessed the glorious antics of Leo Najo.

After leaving the Tulsa Oilers, Najo spent much of his time playing for and managing the Mission 30-30s semi-pro team. It might be said that playing professionally was just a job for Najo, but his involvement with the 30-30s was his passion. The Mission team, which he helped create, was his solace from the often-ruthless environment of the minor leagues. With the 30-30s, he could relax and be himself, associate with younger players who greatly admired him, and just enjoy the game he loved so much.

He served as the team's manager in the 1930s. Friends later recalled that he loved managing the young players on the squad. Abelardo Casas Sr., an outfielder with the 30-30s, said, "When he managed us, he said it was the best years of his life as a manager. He could manage because we would never talk back to him."

"He was very good at giving advice," Casas told a McAllen newspaper. "I used to go to him with a problem, and he'd straighten me out. He'd tell me to do this and do that. He was a very honest man."

Reflecting on his former manager who later became a close friend, Casas added, "He was a very smart manager. He was a good man, smart and very tolerable of us."

LEO NAJO: BASEBALL'S FIRST LATINO SUPERSTAR

In order to understand more fully the life and career of the remarkable Leo Najo, we must also know the incredible story of one of the longest-lived and most successful semi-pro baseball teams in South Texas, the Mission 30-30s, of which Najo was an integral part. In this chapter, we will examine more closely the history of this unique organization.

In 1918, a group of young South Texas baseball enthusiasts, including Leo Najo, dubbed the semi-pro baseball team that they had formed the 30-30s. Spanish-speaking fans referred to them as *La Treinta Treinta*. Named after a popular firearm of the time, the Winchester 30-30 rifle, the team played semi-pro ball on a regular basis from 1919 through 1964. For most of those years, except when away from home playing minor league baseball in the Texas League or the Western League, Najo was involved with the club, first as a player and later as a manager and coach.

According to a 1971 article in the Mission Times, the original members of the 1919 Mission 30-30s were: Leo Najo, Pepe Barrera, Porfirio Guerra, Jose Saenz, Pedro I. Vela, Joe Treda, Taurino Pena, Jesus Saenz, Jacinto Gonzalez and a soldier from Ft. Ringgold named Myers. The organizer of the original team and its first manager was Dario de la Garza, father of Kika de La Garza, a U.S. Congressman from 1965 to 1997, now deceased.

"My father organized the first 30-30 Rifles baseball team," the former Congressman said in a 2005 interview. "Father never played; he just managed. Leo Najo was one of his first players." Two of Kika's uncles, Ramon and Enrique, also played for the 30-30s. "Later, they dropped the *Rifles* part of the name and just called them the 30-30s."

According to De La Garza, his father and Najo were such close friends that when the elder De La Garza got married, he hired Najo to drive him and his bride to San Antonio for their honeymoon. "We always joke that when they got to the hotel room in San Antonio, we aren't sure if they got two rooms or just one, because he and Najo were such good buddies," De La Garza said.

De la Garza said that his family has always been "very proud" of its involvement with the team. He added, "Years later, Leo Najo came to my uncle, Lino Lopez, and told him that the Mission 30-30s ballpark was going to be torn down. Lino agreed to buy it, and we always joke that because of that, Rene Lopez and I got to play on the team."

"During the World War II years, Leo Najo reorganized a young 30-30s team, which I played on," De La Garza said. "I wasn't much good because I couldn't hit. I couldn't see the ball, and it wasn't until later that I realized I needed glasses."

Because Kika was a fast runner, Najo would say to him, "Don't swing the bat. Just get in the way of the ball." De La Garza remembered, "Once I got on base, with my speed, I could steal second, third, home – whatever. I just couldn't hit worth a darn."

De La Garza said that his father's admiration for the team continued long after he stopped managing. "My dad was a great baseball fan. He was there for every game involving the 30-30s."

The photo below, in which the team members are not identified, is of the 1923 team.

The Mission 30-30s in 1923 (Courtesy of Pikey Rodriguez)

According to Dario Garcia of McAllen, who played catcher for the 30-30s in the 1940s and 1950s, the team enjoyed three major "eras." The first era was from its founding in 1918 through the 1920s.

LEO NAJO: BASEBALL'S FIRST LATINO SUPERSTAR

The second era was in the 1930s. The third and final era began in the 1940s and continued into the early 1960s.

Garcia said that the 30-30s played baseball against Monterrey, Reynosa, Laredo, Robstown, the Alamo Wildcats, Pharr, other semipro teams from Mexico, and area teams sponsored by local businesses. "This area was a great baseball area," adds Kika de la Garza. "Mission had the 30-30s. McAllen had the Palms. There were good teams in Donna, Edinburg, Mercedes, San Benito, Harlingen, and Brownsville. We had our own Valley League of semi-pro teams."

According to De La Garza, although the teams consisted mostly of amateur players, the teams did regularly bring in professional players from Mexico and elsewhere, which were added into the mix. "The guys they would bring in from Mexico – a pitcher here or a catcher there – would receive twenty dollars a game, which is why the teams were considered semi-pro."

"I remember my dad bringing in a pitcher named Guayule from Camargo, I think, and my dad paid him twenty dollars a game and all the beer he could drink after the game at Najo's tavern in downtown Mission," De La Garza remembers with a grin. Many of the ball players that were brought in to "guest star" with the 30-30s stayed in a guest room at the home of De La Garza's grandfather. "We only had one little motel in Mission at that time; so, that was the baseball players' room over at my grandfather's house," De La Garza says.

Dario Garcia recalls that the Mission 30-30s used two separate home stadiums over the years. The first ballpark, used in the 1930s, was located on the site now occupied by the city's Ray Landry Fireman's Park. The second park, used in the 1940s and 1950s, was the one located near the corner of Walsh Avenue and Perez Street.

According to Kika de la Garza, Leo Najo often brought the teams that he was playing professionally with to Mission to play the 30-30s. "That was very common with Najo, when he played with other teams. He played with the Alijadores of Tampico, for example, in the Mexican League, and he brought them down here. The Alijadores included some of the greats of Mexican baseball, and the 30-30s beat them in one game."

The 1938 photo that follows shows, kneeling left to right: Gonzalo "El Tonto" Ramirez (Najo's half brother), Erasmo Flores, Tereso

Segovia, Joaquin Castro, and Ramon de la Garza. Standing left to right: Chano Gonzales, Pepe Barrera, Ernesto Flores, Ernesto Contreras, George Stromeyer, and Bernardo Pena.

The Mission 30-30s in 1938 (Courtesy of Pikey Rodriguez)

On April 10, 1938, the 30-30s played an exhibition game against the McAllen Palms of the Class D Texas Valley League. Before the contest, the local newspaper reported, "Ernesto Contreras, Rifles' manager, informed manager Ray Friday of the Palms that he would invade the park with a fast-stepping aggregation of players who are ready to go with three weeks practice under their belts. They will however be without the services of Leo Najo and Octavio Sanchez, who helped build the Rifles club into one of the strongest semi-pro teams in South Texas. The fence busters are now in Palm's uniforms."

With their two strongest players stolen away by the Palms, the 30-30s did not put up much of a fight against the professional team. The one-sided affair, played at McAllen's Legion Park, ended up in a 13-4 victory for the Palms. A local sportswriter blamed the loss on the diminishing skills of Mission's aging pitcher, Bernardo Pena, who was fairly well rocked by the McAllen hitters.

	1	2	3	4	5	6	7	8	9	-	R	H	E
Mission	1	0	0	1	0	1	1	0	0	-	4	5	2
McAllen	4	2	1	4	1	0	1	0	x	-	13	8	2

LEO NAJO: BASEBALL'S FIRST LATINO SUPERSTAR

Former Congressman De La Garza recalled that there were many different "versions" of the Mission 30-30s. "There were the Spikes Motors 30-30s and the Valley Brick 30-30s. The team's name depended on what business was sponsoring them. But even when we didn't have a sponsor, there were still a bunch of guys that would get together and play."

Joe Pompa, an outfielder with the 30-30s from 1947 to 1956, remembers helping to build the Mission 30-30s ballpark at Walsh Avenue and Perez Street. "We built that park in 1947," Pompa says. "All the players pitched in to help build it. My dad was the one who masterminded the building of the stands. We worked from a pattern, built the sections flat, and then stood them up." Businessmen from Mission and McAllen put up the money to build the stadium. "We even put in some of our own money," Pompa adds. The all-wood ballpark was the scene of many memorable baseball games, before it was finally torn down in the early 1970s.

When Pompa started playing with the 30-30s in 1947, Najo was still pinch-hitting for the team on a regular basis. "He still knew how to hit," Pompa notes. "He was still in good shape. He took care of himself."

Among the teams that Pompa, Najo, and the 30-30s faced that year were semi-pros from Brownsville, Harlingen, Pharr, Laredo, and McAllen. From 1946 to 1951, the 30-30s would occasionally also travel to face semi-pro teams from Corpus Christi, Port Arthur, Del Rio, and San Antonio.

Pompa recalls, "We used to play once or twice a week on weekends. We practiced Tuesdays and Fridays after work from five to seven at the stadium. Najo arrived for the practices before we did, and he was right there to make sure we were in shape."

Asked if Najo was very demanding of his players, Pompa answered, "No, he would give us pointers on how to play better, but he wasn't always on us. He believed that the ability to play baseball was something you were born with, and if a guy didn't have it, you couldn't really teach it to him."

"Our team did not play for money," Pompa says. "We played for the sport of it. It was for fun. I remember that we used to barbecue there at the stadium after the games. All the guys would gather together to eat and drink."

One thing Najo never did, according to Pompa, is brag about his own abilities. "People talked good about him, but he never did. Although he was one of the best players ever in San Antonio history, he never talked about himself."

Another footnote in the 1947 team's season is the participation of a Mission youngster named Tom Landry. According to ex-player Dario Garcia, although he did not play for very long, the future Dallas Cowboys coach was a hard-hitting left fielder who made quite an impact on the 1947 team. Garcia said, "I remember a local store was giving away a free watch to the first player who hit a homerun, and Tom Landry got that watch. He was a good player." Dario says.

"He came over on his summer vacation from the University of Texas, and he used to practice with us," says Pompa. "His sport was football, but he wanted to stay in shape; so, he would come over and play with us."

Pompa adds, "He was a pretty good kid. Any position you put him into, he would do well. He was a good guy. Later, when he was playing football with the New York Giants, he would still come down to Mission to see us. He would shake my head, and we would talk about the days when he used to work out with us."

Pompa also remembers a monstrous homerun hit by Landry in the Mission 30-30 ballpark. "He hit a homerun once here in Mission, and he talked about for about three months afterward," Pompa says, grinning.

Kika de la Garza also remembers the future Cowboys coach. "Tom Landry came from U.T. one summer and played for the 30-30s just that one summer. Almost every time he hit, he hit a homer."

Garcia also remembers that on the opening day of the Mission 30-30s season one year in the early 1950s, the governor of Texas, Allan Shivers, threw out the first pitch of the game. De la Garza recalls that Shivers was quite a fan of the Mission 30-30s. "Shivers married John Shary's daughter, and although he was originally from Port Arthur, the Valley was his adopted home. The Sharys were always very supportive of the 30-30s. Not only did Shivers throw out the first ball, but he came to the stadium often to see Mission play, back when he was lieutenant governor and later when he became governor."

The last known photograph of the Mission 30-30s team is from 1954, and it is on display at the Mission Historical Museum. Unfortunately, the team members from 1954 are not identified. By this time, the history of the 30-30s was starting to wind down. The club finally disbanded around 1964.

In the 1947 photo that follows, standing left to right are: Matias Garza, Meme Cavazos, Bill Woods, Walton Gibbs, Rene Lopez, Tom Landry, Ines Pinon, Alfonso "Guayule" Rodriguez, Leo Najo, Aberlardo Casas, and Joe Pompa. Kneeling left to right are: Dario Garcia, Ernesto Flores, Jose Puente, Jose Vasquez, Enrique "Kika" de la Garza, Eduardo "Lefty" Sanchez, and Enrique Moreno.

The Mission 30-30s in 1947. (Courtesy of Pikey Rodriguez)

Reynaldo "Rey" Valadez, who pitched both for Najo and against him in the late 1940s and early 1950s, remembers, "He was still active. He was still good. He was a good hitter. I remember that, even when he was about 50, he would come in as a pinch hitter and could still really smack the ball." According to Valadez, Najo did not appear in games too often, but he would insert himself into the lineup as a pinch hitter "if he had a man in scoring position in the later innings of a game."

Valadez remembers one game in which he was pitching and trying to protect a one-run lead late in the game, when Najo came up to face him as a pinch hitter. Valadez's teammates, all of whom knew Najo well, instructed him on how to pitch to Najo in order to get him out. "They told me not to throw a curve ball to him. They said throw him high fastballs, which because of his age, he won't hit."

Valadez proceeded to get two quick fastball strikes on Najo and then decided to put him away with a curve ball on the outside corner of the plate. "And by golly, he got a hold of that ball and hit it low over second base, but it was starting to rise. The center fielder moved in to catch the ball, but he misjudged it, and it went over his head and to the fence."

One runner scored ahead of him, but Najo, who was in his fifties at the time, was only able to get to third base. He was so winded by the time he reached third that he had to hold on to the third baseman in order to keep himself from falling. In deference to Najo's legendary status, the game's umpire declared a victory for Najo's team, although Leo never actually made it home with the winning run. The umpire later tried to apologize to Valadez, but Rey says he told the umpire, "It's alright with me. Don't worry about it." It was understood that Najo deserved the limelight, even so late in his career.

In a 1971 *Mission Times* photo, Leo Najo appears with a group of former 30-30s players. The caption reads "Some of Leo Najo's long-time baseball compadres gather with the former star and talk over days past with the Mission 30-30s, the best semi-pro team ever fielded in South Texas. From left to right are Ernesto Contreras of McAllen, Jose Garza Carrion of Edinburg, Najo, Pepe Barrera of Mission and Rodolfo Gonzalez of Weslaco. Najo and Barrera were on the original 30-30s team. Other members of that team, organized in 1919, were Porfirio Guerra, Jose Saenz, Pedro I. Vela, Joe Treda, Taurino Pena, Jesus Saenz, Jacinto Gonzalez, and a soldier from Fort Ringgold named Myers. Later 30-30s included Adan Contreras, Dario de la Garza (the original manager), Enrique "Kika" de la Garza, Manuel Guerra, Paul Johnson, Matias "Wild Mate" Garza, Earl Caldwell, Eddie Marburger, Perry Wright, Lyndal Lehman, Herb Melch, Dan Dillard, Julias Grant, Erasmo and Ernesto Flores, Billy Walsh,

LEO NAJO: BASEBALL'S FIRST LATINO SUPERSTAR

George Strohmeyer, Dario Garcia, Rene Solis, Santos Sanchez, Bill and Nick Yoder and Camilo Rodriguez."

In a 1997 newspaper article, Camilo Rodriguez told an interesting story about an incident that occurred while Leo was managing the Mission 30-30s. Mission, whose players were very young and inexperienced, played a game against another young group of semi-pro players from the tiny neighboring town of Madero.

An extremely hard-fought contest ensued, and the score was tied in the ninth inning, when Najo suddenly inserted himself into the 30-30s lineup as a pinch hitter. Relying on his years of experience facing some of the best pitchers in the minors, Najo slammed a base hit to drive home the winning run for Mission.

Following the game, Najo, whose day job was selling and delivering beer to Mission-area taverns, suddenly discovered that the businesses around Madero were no longer buying from him. It turns out that the friends and relatives of the Madero players still deeply resented his decision to put himself into the game. "They thought he was a bully. They had a young team, and they thought he had taken advantage of their young players."

The truth is that the Mission team was also very young, and Najo just got so emotionally involved in the game that he just could not sit back and allow his players to let the victory slip away. This incident spoke more to the strong attachment of Najo to his young players than it did to any use of unfair tactics.

Longtime Rio Grande Valley high school baseball coach Eliseo Pompa, the nephew of Joe Pompa, tells the story of a game in which a pitcher for the 30-30s (believed to be Eduardo "Lefty" Sanchez) was having a terrible outing. Almost every pitch he threw was hit hard to the outfield, and the Mission outfielders were quickly running out of breath from chasing the many balls landing all around them. It seemed that the inning would never end.

After taking a slow walk from the dugout to the mound, manager Najo told the pitcher, "It looks like I'm going to have to take you out. You're just getting too darned tired."

The pitcher reflected for a moment and then said with a perfectly straight face, "Najo, I'm okay. Maybe you need to change the outfielders, because those guys are the ones who are tired."

Najo's involvement with the 30-30s continued through the 1950s. His daughter Alicia says, "I remember going to the baseball stadium in Mission in the 1950s, but by then he was just managing. Every now and then, he would put himself into a game, and the crowd would cheer and go wild. But that didn't happen too often, because he was already in his fifties by then. Can you imagine?"

Chapter 17
The McAllen Palms (1938)

When Najo parted ways with the Tulsa Oilers in 1933, it seemed that his professional baseball career was ended. Tired of the endless bus travel and the long seasons away from home, Leo returned to South Texas anxious to settle into a more relaxed and comfortable lifestyle, centered on his involvement with the Mission 30-30s. He displayed no interest at all in heading north again to endure the grind of another minor league season. But then, a very unusual thing happened. Minor league baseball landed right on his South Texas doorstep.

In 1938, the minor leagues dropped right in Najo's lap with the creation of the Texas Valley League, featuring teams in McAllen, Harlingen, Brownsville, Corpus Christi, Refugio, and Taft. Early in 1938, the *Washington Post* reported that the National Association had just approved the new minor league for the Rio Grande Valley and that games were to begin on April 14, 1938. The Texas Valley League was the first attempt to return professional baseball to South Texas since the failure of the Class D Rio Grande Valley League in 1931.

McAllen, neighboring city to Mission, undoubtedly set its eyes on 39-year-old Leo Najo very early in the planning process for the creation of the McAllen Palms baseball team. An article in *The Sporting News* said, "Organization of the McAllen Baseball Association, which has won a franchise in the recently formed Texas Valley Class D league, was commenced last week with the election of a board of directors. Seven McAllen businessmen form the Association's board…"

Excitement in the new league began building throughout the Rio Grande Valley. Ray Friday, manager of the new McAllen team, held a meeting with athletes from three Hidalgo County high schools. Relying on experience gained in 17 years as a minor league pitcher and coach, Friday gave the attentive high school students pointers on the game. Because of that session, interest in baseball peaked at Valley high schools and, for the first time in ten years, a high school baseball league formed in the Valley for 1938.

Engaged to play centerfield for the McAllen Palms was none other than Leo Najo. Apparently, even after being away from pro ball for six years, Leo could not pass up the opportunity to play the game he loved professionally, while still living at home and without having to travel long distances. Najo's schedule of games with the Palms:

Home vs. Refugio	April 20,21,22; May 13,14,15
	May 13,14,15; June 12,13,14
	Aug 4,5,6,18,19
Home vs. Taft	April 23,24,25; May 25,26,27
	June 21,22,23; July 20,21,22
	Aug 26,27
Home vs. Corpus	April 15,18,19
	June 9,10,11,24,25,26
	July 23,24,25; Aug 20,21
Home vs. Harlingen	May 10,11,12,22,23,24
	June 30; July 1,2,14,15,16
	Aug 14,15
Home vs. Brownsville	May 7,8,9; June 6,7,8
	June 6,7,8; July 3,4,4,11,12,13
	Aug 10,11
Away at Refugio	April 29,30; May 1,19,20,21
	July 5,6,7,29,30,21
	Aug. 22,23
Away at Taft	May 2,3,4,28,29,30
	June 27,28,29
	Aug 7,8,9,24,25
Away at Corpus	April 14,16,17; May 16,17,18
	June 18,19,20; July 26,27,28
	Aug. 28,28
Away at Harlingen	April 26,27,28; May 31
	June 1,2,15,16,17
	July 17,18,19; Aug 12,13
Away at Brownsville	May 5,5,6; June 3,4,5
	July 8,9,10; Aug 1,2,3,16,17

LEO NAJO: BASEBALL'S FIRST LATINO SUPERSTAR

McAllen's newspaper, the *Valley Evening Monitor* said of Najo, "Although the oldest man from the standpoint of experience in both class and minor league ball on the McAllen Palms, Leo Najo is considered the ace of the club's outfielders, and Friday afternoon against Corpus Christi he will be seen out in the centerfield position he played with both the Texas and Western League years ago."

Opening day on Thursday, April 14, 1938 featured Najo and the Palms traveling to Corpus Christi to face the Spudders. Originally scheduled to open at home, McAllen had to move their opener to Corpus Christi due to a conflict with a "circus attraction."

The Spudders quickly turned the game itself into a circus, by pounding out 17 hits and scoring 19 runs en route to a 19-8 victory. Najo started in centerfield and batted third in the lineup. He had two hits, including a double, in four at-bats. The contest lasted two hours and 52 minutes. The game also produced the first homerun of the new season when, in the sixth inning, Corpus second baseman George Hausman cleared the left field wall, 345 feet from home plate. The scoring was:

	1	2	3	4	5	6	7	8	9	-	R	H	E
McAllen	0	0	0	0	1	0	1	3	3	-	8	11	1
Corpus Christi	0	0	1	4	1	4	6	3	x	-	19	17	5

McAllen's season got off to a shaky start, with five straight losses, but the Palms finally broke through on April 20 with a 6-3 win over Refugio. After the first two weeks of play, McAllen held a 1-8 record and occupied last place in the league standings.

On May 5, Najo and the Palms scored 12 runs in the fourth inning of a game against Brownsville to give McAllen a 22-15 victory. On May 9, the Palms played their first night game ever at their home park against the hapless Brownsville club. In a rare three-hour game that featured 45 hits, the Charros upset the Palms 30-11 to spoil their night debut.

Rumors began to circulate that the McAllen franchise was in financial trouble and might cease operations. A note in *The Sporting News* said: "Fears that the McAllen franchise would be forfeited have been allayed by the decision of the offices of the McAllen Baseball

Association to continue operations. A meeting was held with League President Guy Alroy, following reports of disbandment, and businessmen responded by pledging their support to the club."

On May 17, McAllen lost 25-13 to Corpus Christi in a game that saw 43 hits, 13 errors, and 12 walks. The official scorer may have taken the worst of the beating, though, as for the final three innings of the game, the McAllen players, with a victory hopelessly out of reach, suddenly began moving from position to position "in utter abandon." Two days later, Leo Najo and the Palms beat Refugio, 7-1.

A day after the Refugio game, the struggling Palms accepted the resignation of their manager, Ray Friday. McAllen then hired their catcher, Wally Kopp, as player-manager.

In an effort to drum up support for the Palms among longtime Valley baseball fans, May 22 was declared "Leo Najo Day" at American Legion Park. The local paper reported, "If the advance dope is any indication of what the size of the crowd will be for the McAllen Palms-Harlingen Hubs double-bill feature here Sunday afternoon in honor of Leo Najo, Palms centerfield, then Legion Park doesn't have the seating accommodations."

The article continued, "McAllen Baseball Association officials expect 2,500 persons to attend the games, which have been dedicated 'Leo Najo Day' in tribute to the speedy little mid-fielder, who at the age of 39 is making an outstanding comeback in professional baseball after a 10-year absence from the pro diamonds."

A crowd of 1,800 attended Leo's big night, and although the man of honor was originally not scheduled to play, he did end up playing one inning in left field, and he also pinch-hit once. The Palms lost the first game of the doubleheader 12-10 but came back to win the second game 7-5.

With their new manager and an influx of new players, McAllen sought to improve its fortunes as the first half wound to a close. Najo's team won four out of their first five games after the managerial change. On May 31, pitcher Jack Griggs, obtained from the East Texas League, led McAllen to a 9-4 win over Harlingen. The Palms moved over to Brownsville on June 4, where they defeated the Charros, 1-0. On June 9, McAllen blistered Harlingen 10-0 behind the torrid hitting of third baseman Campbell McClanahan, who pounded out three homeruns in the game. At this point in the season, two McAllen Palms were tied for most homeruns in the league – Leo Najo and Kirby Jordan, each with seven homers.

On June 13, Najo blasted two homeruns as McAllen mounted an 18-hit attack to defeat Refugio, behind the six-hit pitching of Clyde Chisum, who struck out seven Oilers. Despite their success on the field, the McAllen club continued to suffer financially. *The Sporting News* reported, "Facing financial difficulties and possible abandonment of their club, McAllen club officials announced, June 14, the team would be able to finish the season with the receipt of two checks from a couple of 'angels,' whose identifies, at their own request, were not revealed."

On June 18, Leo Najo broke up a no-hitter attempt by Corpus Christi pitcher Homer Gibson. Najo's single off Gibson was the only McAllen hit in a 5-0 loss.

On June 21, the halfway point of the season arrived with Corpus Christi maintaining a lead on Harlingen in a very close race. The standings showed:

Team	*W*	*L*	*Pct*
Corpus Christi	49	18	.731
Harlingen	41	27	.603
Taft	36	29	.554
Refugio	33	34	.493
McAllen	27	41	.397
Brownsville	14	51	.215

The Palms got a great start on the first day of the second half of the season. McAllen won both ends of a doubleheader 16-13 and 12-8 over Taft on June 22. In fact, McAllen played .600 ball in their first 35 games of the second half. On June 27, Najo and the Palms got 20 hits in defeating Taft, 17-7.

Pacing the McAllen club was Leo Najo's continued excellent hitting. On July 19, Najo pounded a game winning homerun to defeat Harlingen 7-6. The Palms had opened the series in Harlingen on July 17 with a 3-2 victory over the Hubs. On July 21, Najo's infield mate, second baseman Ray Taylor, drove in eight runs, including four on a homerun, as the Palms defeated Taft, 9-4.

On July 23, Najo hit an eighth-inning homerun with two men on base to climax a five-run rally that gave McAllen a 9-6 advantage over league-leading Corpus Christi. To preserve the victory, Najo made two sensational catches in centerfield in the top of the ninth. One of the catches was an *outfielder's dream*, as Najo leaped onto the outfield fence and made a one-handed grab of a ball that had already been announced as a homerun.

On July 26, second-place Harlingen was McAllen's next victim, suffering a 15-6 defeat at the hands of the Palms. A visiting New York Yankees scout, Joe Devine, was so impressed with what he saw in McAllen and elsewhere in the Texas Valley League that he predicted that within two years the Lower Rio Grande Valley, with its 22 towns and total population of 350,000, would develop into the "hottest" baseball area in the nation.

Najo and the Palms suffered a disappointing loss on July 30 against Refugio in a wild game that featured a combined total of 30 base hits, including 11 doubles and six homeruns. The final score was Refugio 19 and McAllen 12.

On August 6, 1938, the first radio broadcast of an organized baseball game from the Rio Grande Valley took place in McAllen, sponsored by the city's Junior Chamber of Commerce. The radio audience listened intently as Leo Najo drove in a run with a single in the bottom of the ninth inning; unfortunately, it was McAllen's only run of the evening, as the Palms lost 1-5 to Refugio. Nonetheless, the first radio broadcast signaled the intrusion of the media into a sport that previously had been available only to live audiences. The future would soon bring a saturation of the airwaves with baseball, declining attendance at games, and a severe downturn in the fortunes of the nation's minor league teams.

The Palms reeled off 14 straight victories through August 21, but their efforts to move up to fourth place and ensure themselves a spot in the playoffs fell just a little bit short.

Najo finished the season as the seventh best hitter in the league with a batting average of .354. In 367 at-bats for the McAllen Palms, Najo had 130 hits, including 20 homeruns, 28 doubles, and five triples. He scored 106 runs, stole 19 bases, sacrificed 22 times, drew 90 bases on balls, and drove in 91 runs. The statistics were quite impressive for a 39-year-old man who had not played professionally in six years. When league play ended on August 28, the standings were:

Team	W	L	Pct
Corpus Christi	92	44	.677
Harlingen	84	53	.613
Taft	30	26	.536
Refugio	67	67	.500
McAllen	65	72	.474
Brownsville	30	103	.226

Defensively, Najo had an amazing 229 putouts with 11 assists and only six errors. His fielding percentage of .976 ranked him as the 10th best defensive outfielder in the league.

After the season, the press bureau of the National Association of Professional Baseball Leagues selected an all-star team. Najo received honorable mention.

Texas Valley League officials, despite the financial difficulties experienced by some its clubs, publicly expressed their intent to return in 1939. In November 1938, league officials said that all six Texas Valley clubs planned to return and that the league might add teams from Mission, Mercedes, and San Benito to the circuit.

Chapter 18
The Mexican League Years (1939-1940)

Leo Najo's outstanding performance in the 1938 Texas Valley League proved to himself and to others that even at age 39, he was still an outstanding ballplayer and could make a substantial contribution to any ball club. His year with the McAllen Palms had whetted his appetitive for pro baseball.

Early in 1939, organizers of the Texas Valley League discussed the possibility of adding one or more teams from Mexico, thus creating the first international minor league. Among the Mexican cities said to be interested in joining were Monterrey, Mexico City, and Tampico.

According to an article in *The Sporting News* on March 30, 1939, the National Association of Professional Baseball Leagues had already granted permission for the inclusion of up to two Mexican teams in the Texas Valley League. The article said that McAllen, Brownsville, Harlingen, Corpus Christi, and Laredo were already aboard for the league's 1939 season, but a sixth team was needed, and it would likely be one from Mexico.

All three Mexican cities mentioned as candidates already had teams playing in the independent Mexican League. In 1939, Monterrey had a team called "Carta Blanca," named after the popular Mexican beer. Mexico City a team called the "Comintra." Tampico had the "Alijadores."

In the early 1920s, Leo Najo had played baseball for a team in Tampico and for Cuauhtemoc of Monterrey. He likely followed with great interest the discussions in early 1939 about bringing a team from Mexico into the Texas Valley League.

Unfortunately for Najo and for South Texas, all the talk about a 1939 season for the Texas Valley League ended in bitter disappointment. An April 13 front-page story in *The Sporting News*

LEO NAJO: BASEBALL'S FIRST LATINO SUPERSTAR

said that previous reports of the Texas Valley League continuing in 1939 were "a fabrication of words and nothing more."

Perhaps the biggest reason for the league's failure, a Brownsville sports editor later wrote, was the lack of lighted fields. Sports editor Ken Johnson wrote, "Summer afternoons were just too hot to attract crowds to a baseball game and a limited number of fans could get away to watch the game regardless of the weather."

With the demise of the Texas Valley League, Leo Najo turned his attention to the possibility of playing professionally in Mexico. It is uncertain whether he made the initial contact with team officials in Tampico, or whether they sought him out. In any event, Najo decided to return to professional baseball as a player-manager for the Tampico Alijadores in 1939.

Najo (right) in Tampico, 1939. (Courtesy of Athit Farias)

According to *The Encyclopedia of Minor League Baseball*, baseball in Mexico became "organized" in 1937 when twelve teams banded together to form the independent Mexican League. The league featured teams from Veracruz, Cordoba, Nogales, Mexico City, Santa

Rosa, Tampico, and Rio Blanco. Five teams from Mexico City competed in that inaugural year, which consisted of a very modest 25-game schedule for each team. Veracruz (20-4) won the 1937 Mexican League championship by downing the Mexico City Agrario (21-4), three games to none. Tampico finished fourth in the South Division.

In 1938, while Leo Najo was playing for the Texas Valley League, the Mexican League, now trimmed down to just eight teams, expanded its schedule to about 50 games per club. Veracruz (40-9) again finished atop the league standings. Tampico finished third.

For the 1939 season, the Mexican League dropped to seven teams and expanded its schedule to about 60 games per club. At the start of the season, the teams and their managers were announced:

Team	*Manager*
Anahuac Indios	Chucho Castillo
Cordoba Cafeteros	Lazaro Salazar
Mexico City Comintra	Manuel Oliveros
Monterrey Carta Blanca	Guillermo Ornelas
Santa Rosa Gallos	Leonardo Olvera
Tampico Alijadores	Leonardo Alanis (Leo Najo)
Veracruz Aguila	Augustin Verde

It is important to note that in this era, U.S. baseball officials considered the Mexican League to be an "outlaw" circuit. Until Mexican baseball officials signed agreements with Major League Baseball in the 1950s, the Mexican League was viewed with great suspicion. Mexican team owners often lured away players from the United States, especially from the Negro Leagues, to play south of the border. In 1938, for example, the league's leading hitter was U.S. Hall of Fame pitcher Martin Dihigo.

Many baseball historians consider Martin Dihigo to have been the most versatile player in baseball history. Known as "El Maestro," the native of Cuba played all nine positions skillfully. Dihigo was a star wherever he played, including Cuba, Mexico, Puerto Rico, Venezuela, and the U.S. Negro leagues, where he spent 12 seasons. Dihigo is a member of the baseball halls of fame in the United States, Cuba, and Mexico. Playing as a pitcher for Veracruz in 1938, he went

LEO NAJO: BASEBALL'S FIRST LATINO SUPERSTAR

18-2 and led the league with a 0.90 ERA, while also winning the batting crown with a .387 mark.

Apart from its "outlaw" reputation, the Mexican League was also a place where "over-the-hill" American baseball players could extend their professional careers by a few more years. Many older players who were either unable or unwilling to make money doing anything else, headed across the border to play for baseball-starved fans throughout Mexico.

Into this environment, in 1939, went Leo Najo of Mission, Texas, who played professionally in Mexico under his birth name of "Leonardo Alanis." At age 40, Najo began his new job with the Tampico Alijadores. In part, he was reliving fond memories from his youth, of when he had first played baseball in Tampico. From Tampico's perspective, the team was getting a major league caliber player who had just finished an outstanding season in the Texas Valley League the year before.

With Najo playing and managing, Tampico had an excellent season. The team was led by power hitting first baseman Angel Castro, who led the league with nine homeruns and 50 runs-batted-in. Castro, a native Mexican, went on to become one of the greatest players in the early history of the Mexican League. Castro's career spanned 20 years, and he was elected to the Mexican baseball hall of fame in 1964.

As player-manager, Najo himself took the field during the 1939 season, compiling a batting average of .259. He also hit three homeruns and drove in eleven runs in the league's short season.

After their 55 games, Najo's team won 30 and lost 25 for a .545 winning percentage. Though they did very well, the Alijadores finished 14 ½ games out of first place.

Many years later, reflecting on his experiences as manager of Tampico, Najo confided to one of his Mission ballplayers, Abelardo Casas, Sr., that managing in Tampico had not been altogether pleasant. Casas said, "He told me once he managed in Mexico for Tampico, but he wasn't very good at it because they were all stars from Cuba and all other parts. He couldn't manage them with satisfaction. He couldn't put his ideas out there. They all considered themselves stars."

Two former stars of the U.S. Negro leagues, Agustin Bejerano and Lazaro Salazar, both Cubans, led the Cordoba Cafeteros to the 1939 league championship. Bejerano led the league with 81 hits on the season, and Salazar had the highest batting average (.374) and had the most wins as a pitcher (16).

The league's final standings showed:

Team	W	L	Pct	GB
Cordoba Cafeteros	46	12	.793	--
Veracruz Aguila	37	21	.638	9
Tampico Alijadores	30	25	.545	14 ½
Anahuac Indios	31	28	.525	15 ½
Monterrey Carta Blanca	31	29	.517	16
Mexico City Comintra	16	41	.281	29 ½
Santa Rosa Gallos	11	46	.193	34 ½

Second-place Veracruz was again led by pitcher Martin Dihigo, who led the league in strikeouts with 202. Another strong player for Veracruz was screwball pitcher Barney Brown, a Negro leaguer who was once called "the Warren Spahn of the Negro Leagues."

Another very noteworthy event happened in 1939 for Leo Najo. In a poll of Mexican baseball fans conducted by Mexico City's daily sports publication *La Afición*, Najo was one of only five players chosen for inclusion in the first group selected to the Mexican Professional Baseball Hall of Fame.

Baseball writer Jesse Sanchez later wrote, "The first class elected in 1939 by the fans were Lucas *El Indio* Juárez, Antonio Delfín *Lañiza*, Julio Molina *El Diamante Blanco*, Leonardo *Najo* Alanís, and Fernando *Cocuite* Barradas. They were honored with bronze plaques at Delta Park in Mexico City during the 1940s."

Najo's career had come full circle. Born in Mexico, he had played professionally in Mexico as a youth before his illustrious career in the U.S. minor leagues. Now, as his playing days were near an end, he had received the ultimate honor that any Mexican baseball player could have.

After his year in Tampico and his selection to Mexican baseball's Hall of Fame, Najo decided to play one more year in the Mexican

LEO NAJO: BASEBALL'S FIRST LATINO SUPERSTAR

League. He signed on to play for the Mexico City Diablo Rojos ("Red Devils") in 1940. The *Professional Baseball Player Database* lists individual player statistics for him for 1940 as a member of the Diablo Rojos.

Although 1940 was their inaugural season, the Diablo Rojos went on to build a long and storied history that continues today. The team was founded by Ernesto Carmona, who became the team's first manager, and Salvador Lutteroth. Carmona was famous in Mexico as the man who created the very first professional baseball league in Mexico in 1925. In the 1940s, Carmona and his pal Jorge Pasquel, attempted a transformation of Mexican baseball to make it more like the U.S. major leagues. Carmona is credited for turning the Mexico City Diablos Rojos into one of the most popular and enduring professional sports franchises in the history of Mexico.

In 1940, in addition to managing the Mexico City team, Carmona assumed the role of league president. The Mexican League also welcomed several new teams and cities, and the playing schedule was expanded to about 90 games. The teams and managers for the new season were:

Team	*Manager*
Chihuahua Dorados	Sergio Correa
Mexico City Diablos Rojos	Ernesto Carmona
Monterrey Industriales	Jose Luis Gomez
Nuevo Laredo Tecolotes	Stanley Pintorell
Tampico Alijadores	Guillermo Ornelas
Torreon Algodoneros	Matanzas Valdez
Veracruz Azules	Martin Dihigo

Veracruz's outstanding Cuban pitcher, Martin Dihigo, took over as the team's manager in 1940, and Veracruz added another Cuban-born star to its roster, pitcher Ramon Bragana. Also of note was the addition of 37-year-old James "Cool Papa" Bell to the roster of the Torreon Algodoneros. One of the greatest players in the history of the Negro leagues, Bell was known for his incredible speed as a base runner, his effectiveness as a lead-off hitter and his outstanding defense as an outfielder. A Hall of Famer in the U.S., Bell played in the Negro leagues for 20 years, with teams such as the St. Louis Stars, Pittsburgh Crawfords and the Homestead Grays.

In 1940, James "Cool Papa" Bell led the Mexican League in batting average (.437), hits (167), runs-batted-in (79), and homeruns (12). Without much of a supporting cast, his team, the Torreon Algodoneros, ended the season at 45-41 and in fifth place in the league.

Playing for Mexico City, Leo Najo compiled a batting average of .294. He hit no homeruns and had only one run-batted-in. Najo's team finished second in the Mexican League, as shown in the final standings:

Team	W	L	Pct	GB
Veracruz Azules	61	30	.670	--
Mexico City Diablos Rojos	57	38	.633	6
Monterrey Industriales	52	41	.559	9
Tampico Alijadores	46	41	.529	13
Torreon Algodoneros	45	41	.523	13 ½
Nuevo Laredo Tecolotes	30	48	.448	24 ½
Chihuahua Dorados	14	67	.173	42

Although Mexico City finished second in the final standings, Najo's team actually beat Veracruz 11 out of the 18 times that the two teams played each other during the season. At one point in the season, Mexico City won 15 games in a row. In one of the outstanding games of the season, Mexico City, with Negro leagues pitcher Theolic "Fireball" Smith on the mound, overcame an outstanding pitching performance by Martin Dihigo to defeat Veracruz, 3-1. Theolic Smith finished the 1940 season with a 19-9 record, and an earned-run-average of 3.49. Only Bill Jefferson of Monterrey, a fellow Negro leagues pitcher, had more victories (22) than Smith.

Following his stint with Mexico City, Leo Najo's time as a professional ball player was ended. Though upon his return to Mission, Najo continued his association with the Mission 30-30s, his playing days were essentially over. He spent his remaining years managing, coaching, umpiring, and generally promoting the game of baseball in South Texas. A photo of the 1947 Mission 30-30s club, on display at the Mission Historical Museum, shows Najo among the members of the team. Also shown on the squad is Tom Landry, future coach of the Dallas Cowboys who was a student at the University of Texas at Austin in 1947.

Reflecting on the end of his career as a player, Najo later told a McAllen newspaper reporter, "Baseball was my life. I lived for the game. Baseball was good to me."

Chapter 19
El Gran Najo Settles Down (1944)

After the annulment of his marriage to Lucy Herrera in the mid-1930s, Najo remained single for a number of years. As Lucy had been unable to have children, Najo's personal life revolved around other members of his family, including his brother and sister. Though he remained emotionally attached to Lucy for years after their separation, Leo desired to have a family of his own, especially as he reached his forties.

Najo (center) in 1947. (Courtesy of Pikey Rodriguez)

Thus it was that in the early 1940s, Najo fell in love with Elida Garza, a Mission teenager whose family lived in one of Leo's rental homes. Leo's granddaughter Athit Farias tells the interesting story of how Leo and Elida came together. Najo showed up in front of Elida's residence at the start of every month to collect the rent. He would stand out in front of the house, chanting the single word "money" in a rather peculiar sort of cadence, and Elida's family would often send her out with the rent money to pay Leo.

LEO NAJO: BASEBALL'S FIRST LATINO SUPERSTAR

One month in the mid-1940s, as Elida approached Leo with the rent, he did not take the money but instead grasped her hand in his. Athit says that Elida averted her eyes from him and was quite embarrassed by the incident. After all, this was the great Leo Najo that everyone in Mission respected so much! Much to her awe and amazement, Leo calmly informed her that he had chosen her to be his wife.

Although some in Elida's family may have raised eyebrows about the couple's age difference, any doubts were quickly overshadowed by Najo's legendary status as a famous baseball player. In a 2005 interview with the author, Elida said, "When I first met him, I knew he was a famous person, but I didn't really know why."

Elida says that Leo was always friendly to her when he came around collecting the rent and also when the two saw each other at a neighborhood store where they both shopped. He did not talk much, but he was clearly interested in her. "He was a very quiet person," Elida said. "He never said anything unless you asked him. If he liked your question, he would answer. If not, he wouldn't."

As a young woman without much interest in sports, she did not understand why Leo was so famous. "I didn't know he had been a famous player. All I knew was that he played ball. I didn't pay much attention to it." She does, however, remember seeing long lines of people walking across the railroad tracks toward the 30-30s ballpark. "It was like a parade," she recalls. "I asked my mom what is was, and she told me that Najo was playing and that all those people were lining up to see him play."

Elida recalls a day when her mother told her that Najo had been hurt while playing baseball with the 30-30s and that he had to be carried off the field. When Elida reacted with indifference to the announcement, her mother scolded her, "You ought to care about it, because he is always around here asking about you."

Finally, the day came when Najo got up the courage to ask her out. Elida remembers that she replied, "Well, I can't, because my father is very strict, and I'm scared of him."

At that time, Elida was working as a waitress for a restaurant in the adjoining town of Edinburg. Early each morning, she would ride the bus from downtown Mission to her place of employment. Leo

Najo began accompanying her on her morning walk to the bus stop, offering her a ride to work in his car. She was not eager to accept the favor, but he was persistent over the course of several days, and one day, he even got on the bus with her and accompanied her all the way to Edinburg.

"I remember thinking that this guy wasn't going to leave me alone," Elida says. "Maybe I ought to just do what he wanted."

On another occasion, Elida was working the night shift at a Mission cannery, when Leo began paying her nocturnal visits. One night, Leo sat outside the plant and waited until 7 a.m. when her shift ended in order to ask her out. "He asked me to go out with him, and we started going out," she says.

Elida's girlfriends told her, "He looks old enough to be your grandfather," but she continued seeing Leo, falling deeply in love with him. Still, the relationship was not without its bumps, as Elida began hearing rumors that Leo was quite the ladies' man around town. She warned him that she would not put up with it. When Elida saw Leo talking to another woman out in front of his tavern one evening, she became very angry.

Elida's family was planning to migrate to Michigan that summer to work as farm laborers, and although she had meant to stay because of Leo, she made a last-second decision to leave with the family in order to teach Najo a lesson about seeing other women. It was a plan that backfired on her, because, shortly after arriving in Michigan, Elida discovered that she was pregnant.

Thousands of miles away from home, living in a crowded shanty without a telephone, Elida was desperate. She needed to find a way to get in touch with Najo and persuade him to take her back. "I was really scared," she remembers. "It seemed impossible." The only thing she could think of was to write him a letter and plead with him to forgive her and to send her money to go back home and be with him.

Her letter reached Leo, and shortly thereafter, Elida was reunited with him in Mission. They remained together from then until Leo's death in 1978. "He was a wonderful husband," Elida says fondly. "We loved each other very much, right up to the end, when I was with him on his deathbed."

LEO NAJO: BASEBALL'S FIRST LATINO SUPERSTAR

Early in their relationship, Leo told Elida that his first wife, Lucy, had convinced him that he was unable to have children. Elida quickly dispelled that notion, as she bore him eleven children, six sons and five daughters. The sons were Leonardo Jr., Rene Roque, Jesse, Alberto, Jose Luis, and Alfredo. The daughters were Maria Guadalupe, Maria Rosario "Chayo," Alicia America, Sylvia, and Linda Yvonne.

Elida was plunged so quickly into the role of mother that she had very little time to worry about discovering more about her husband's legendary baseball career. She recalls, "I didn't know that much about his past baseball career, because I was always busy with the children, and also, he never really said much about it."

Elida remembers once early in their marriage when Najo took her a newspaper clipping and said to her, "Look what is says here about me." Elida read it and was amazed at the extent to which the world of professional baseball looked up to her husband. "It was very emotional," she says. But, after that one lapse, he never really spoke about his career in the minor leagues again until the early 1970s when he was chosen as the first player to be inducted into Mexico's professional baseball hall of fame.

Elida says, "It wasn't until the early 1970s when he was inducted into the Mexican Baseball Hall of Fame and the city named the baseball stadium and a street after him that he finally told us more about his career in the minors. I remember that it was so emotional for all of us. I even got sick and had to go to the hospital, because I got so excited about it."

Elida says of Leo, "He was a good husband, a good father, and a good friend. He was good with the kids. He was a hard worker. He loved to spend time with the kids. He was always buying things for them. He took them to church. He helped them with their homework. He was very close to them. He was just crazy about his children. He adored them."

"He would take the girls to Austin and San Antonio so that they could buy the latest fashions. He was very particular about the clothes that he would buy for them. He took them window shopping often."

Daughter Alicia also remembers the family shopping trips to San Antonio. "We would do a lot of window-shopping. He told us to look at the clothes that the mannequins in the stores were wearing, and he wanted us to dress that way."

Najo's children and grandchildren also have very fond memories of their legendary relative. His daughter Chayo recalls that her father always taught her not to let her gender get in the way of athletic achievement. "He would always have me compete with my brothers," she said. "He wanted me to run faster, jump farther, and be able to transfer one movement to another without any hesitation." According to Chayo, her father told her sometime in the 1950s or early 1960s, "You will be faced with tremendous challenges. You live in a world that is powered by men. You will be the generation that will prove that a woman can do the same job a man is able to do and probably better."

Najo, Circa 1950s (Courtesy of Alicia Farias)

Najo's lessons to Chayo extended beyond the field of play and her future employment. As a person with a scarce formal education himself, Leo pushed his children to excel in school. Chayo remembers, "My grades were good, but not good enough. Mediocrity was unacceptable."

Najo's granddaughter Athit experienced similar teachings. A favorite of Najo, he gave Athit the nickname *Reina*, which is Spanish for *queen*. "As a child, my male cousins wouldn't let me play ball with them, because I was a girl," Athit says, "I remember that Grandfather would pick my head up by the chin, look me straight in the eyes, and say that I should never to let anyone tell me that I can't do something just because I am a girl." Leo then said to her, "Now go out there and show them how to play ball, Reina."

Though she was very young at the time and did not know about Najo's baseball past, Athit later came to understand that Najo's words to her about no quitting came from his own bitter struggles to overcome poverty and racism en route to becoming one of the earliest Latino ballplayers in the United States. "My very first life lessons came not just from my grandfather's heart, but more from his life experiences," she says.

Najo's daughter, Alicia, recalls that her father often seemed demanding, and she questioned why Leo would take the family away as migrant workers to toil in faraway fields. She says, "We would always go to work in the fields, and we wondered why he wanted us to do that. We didn't have to do that, but it was his way of teaching us discipline and the value of an education. He made us realize that if we didn't want to work in the field, we needed to finish our education. That's what he wanted."

Chapter 20
The Rio Grande Valley League (1950)

In 1949, the Class D Rio Grande Valley League began operations and experienced a highly successful first year of league play, featuring teams in McAllen, Brownsville, Donna (later moved to Robstown), Laredo, Del Rio, and Corpus Christi. Although Leo Najo, now 50 years old, was not involved in the league during its first year, he most likely watched its progress with great interest.

McAllen (70-68) and Brownsville (75-65) both made the playoffs but were defeated by the eventual league champions, the Corpus Christi Aces (89-51). The team from Laredo (80-60), nicknamed the Apaches, finished second in the final standing, but was defeated in the semifinals by Brownsville.

Following the 1949 season, league president William R. Byrd announced that the National Association had granted his request for the league to move up to the higher Class C for 1950. Not surprisingly, Leo Najo became involved in the new league, agreeing to become the manager of the 1950 Laredo Apaches. The teams and team officials announced at the start of the season were:

Club	President	Manager
Brownsville Charros	W. W. Ely	Joe King
Corpus Christi Aces	George Schepps	John (Red) Davis
Del Rio Cowboys	Arturo C. Gonzalez	Robert Hamric
Donna-Weslaco Twins	M. L. Wilkison	G. (Baldy) Quinn
Harlingen Capitols	Lloyd Yarbrough	Sam Harshaney
Laredo Apaches	Nick Canavati	L. (Najo) Alaniz
McAllen "Valley" Giants	Logan Drye	Boyd SoRelle
Robstown Rebels	K. B. Morgan	Fabian Kowalik

To his position as field manager of the Laredo Apaches, Najo brought his many years of playing experience in the minors, the majors, and semi-pro ball. Najo also had experience managing the Mission 30-30s and the Tampico ball club. With Leo at the helm,

LEO NAJO: BASEBALL'S FIRST LATINO SUPERSTAR

Apache fans were expecting another strong season like the 65-30 campaign of 1949.

On April 11, the Apaches opened the season at home on an ominous note – a power failure delayed their game for over an hour. Still, the Apaches took advantage of wildness by the Del Rio Cowboys pitcher and four Del Rio fielding errors en route to a 7-4 victory. The box score was:

	1	2	3	4	5	6	7	8	9	-	R	H
Del Rio	0	0	0	0	2	0	1	1	0	-	4	11
Laredo	0	0	0	2	0	1	4	0	x	-	7	7

After the first two weeks of play, the Apaches had put together a good start to the season, going 8-5. As everyone believed he would, Leo Najo was doing an excellent job as the team's manager. The league standings were:

Team	W	L	Pct
Corpus Christi	10	4	.714
Del Rio	9	5	.643
Laredo	8	5	.615
Harlingen	8	5	.615
Brownsville	8	7	.533
Robstown	6	9	.400
McAllen	4	8	.333
Donna-Weslaco	3	13	.188

Meanwhile, the Donna-Weslaco team lost 16 of their first 20 games and suffered terribly low attendance at their home games. Following their game on Thursday, May 4, the team was dissolved, leaving the Rio Grande Valley League with only seven teams.

After the failure of the Donna-Weslaco franchise, speculation arose that one other team would soon be eliminated in order to balance the schedule. When speculation arose that Harlingen, the newest team in the league, was a candidate for removal, league president William R. Byrd stated that Harlingen was financially the healthiest club in the league and was not in jeopardy.

Regarding the Rio Grande Valley League's continued financial problems, one team owner told reporters, "We're sick and tired of trying out every city, town, and whistle-stop in this part of the state to determine whether it will support a franchise." Looking forward to the future of the league, the owners discussed phasing out weak franchises and only keeping the clubs in communities that had proven their ability to support minor league baseball. Owners felt that Corpus Christi, Harlingen, Brownsville, and Laredo were the most likely teams to survive into 1951.

One week later, the league's board of directors, meeting in Del Rio, voted to shut down the Robstown Rebels due to ongoing financial difficulties and poor attendance. The league was now down to just six clubs.

Seeking to explain the problems in South Texas, minor league president George M. Trautman told reporters, "Many organizations in the smaller minors ... are dependent upon the gate to meet their payrolls, being operated on a pay-as-you-go basis, with little reserve cash, and several clubs are reported to be running on narrow margins. Attendance at games which have been played also is low, as compared to last year, the weather being blamed in some quarters and radio and television in others." Trautman warned league presidents to monitor their teams for signs of weakness and impending collapse, and to intervene to prevent more failures with strategies such as promotions aimed at increasing attendance. He added that the effects of radio and television major league broadcasts on minor league attendance were still being studied, but that he felt the majors' broadcasting contracts were "conceived in a spirit of selfishness, in a spirit far removed from the recognition of the rights of minor league clubs."

Although Najo's Laredo team was doing quite well through the end of May, an incident totally unrelated to baseball brought an end to Najo's tenure as the team's manager. According to his wife Elida, Leo was feeling increasingly isolated from his wife and children as the baseball season progressed, despite his efforts to remain connected. When the Laredo team traveled to the Valley to play, Najo would have the bus driver stop by his home so that he could visit with his family. Elida remembers that the first time Leo arrived on the team bus, the children rushed out excitedly to greet him. However, on subsequent visits, Leo noticed that their eagerness to see him was progressively less.

Disturbed that his return to professional baseball was straining his relationship with his wife and children, Najo decided to quit as the Apache manager. "When he arrived on the team bus one day, and the children didn't even come out to see him, he decided it was time to quit. He did not want the children to forget him," his wife recalls. After leaving the Apaches, Najo's only involvement with baseball was his continuing association with the Mission 30-30s.

When Najo departed Laredo at the end of May 1950, the Rio Grande Valley League standings were:

Team	*W*	*L*	*Pct*
Harlingen	32	16	.667
Corpus Christi	30	15	.657
Laredo	26	22	.542
Brownsville	24	25	.440
Del Rio	23	25	.479
McAllen	17	28	.378

Even as Najo was ending his last job in minor league baseball, there were already indications that the Rio Grande League was in trouble and might eventually fold. As it turned out, after Najo left, the league managed to limp along through the rest of the season, but trouble was definitely on the horizon. After the season, *The Sporting News* reported, "Nick Canavati [Laredo's owner] might carry out his threat to put Laredo in the Mexican League."

In the end, Laredo, Harlingen, Brownsville, and Corpus Christi abandoned the Rio Grande Valley League and moved over to the Class B Gulf Coast League for the 1951 season. In January of 1951, the Rio Grande Valley League officially voted to cease operations.

With his departure from the Rio Grande Valley League of 1950, Leo Najo never again participated in a minor league game either as a player or manager. Although he continued to manage and coach for the Mission 30-30s through the 1960s, his long involvement with professional baseball had ended, and this time it was final.

Chapter 21
Baseball's South Texas Ambassador (1951-1978)

Vicente Estevis of Edinburg, who played for Leo Najo on the Mission 30-30s, told the *San Antonio Express-News* in April 2000, "He was a very unassuming and modest man. The thing that stands out the most in my mind is how much he tried to help younger players. He would spend all the time they needed giving tips, advice, whatever. He was an ambassador of the game on both sides of the border."

"He's the one who taught us how to hit when we were in high school," remembers Rey Valadez, another former player. "He used to come to the school during practice, and the coach would let him work with us on our hitting. It was because of him that we learned how to hit."

A 1971 editorial in the *Mission Times* expounded further on the retired legend: "Those who followed baseball 40 or so years ago know they are the chosen ones; for they got to see Leo Najo in his prime. They saw him make sensational catches in the outfield; hit homeruns; walk and then steal second, third, and home on successive pitches."

The article continued, "These old-timers can be forgiven if a tear comes in their eye at the thought that never again will they see Leo Najo run with the grace of a frisky young deer. But those memories are lasting, those memories from a different time, a different world."

After his last season in organized baseball in 1950, Najo spent his time in the Mission area working with both the Mission 30-30s and with local Little League teams. He became so involved with teaching baseball skills to the youth of the Rio Grande Valley that he received a number of awards and proclamations from local city officials.

In 1971, the city of Mission issued a proclamation stating, "Since his retirement from active playing, he has given considerably of his time and talent to instructing and assisting the youth of his hometown." The neighboring city of La Joya commended Najo for dedicating a great deal of his life to the sport of baseball and for spending "much of his time coaching, helping and inspiring our youth to become good baseball players."

Although retired from playing, Najo was often called to participate in baseball events, especially relating to his career in the minor leagues. In one such event, on July 31, 1957, at age 58, Leo played in a scheduled three-inning game between two teams comprised of Texas League "old timers." The game was played at Mission Stadium in San Antonio, prior to the start of a Texas League game between San Antonio and Tulsa.

The game ended in a scoreless tie after the second inning because the teams "ran out of gas," according to one media report. With several players in their fifties and sixties, it was not surprising. "My eyes aren't as good as they once were," said one player.

In September of 1971, "Leo Najo Day" was proclaimed in South Texas, and a huge celebration in his honor was held in Mission and in the neighboring Mexican city of Reynosa. As part of the festivities, the street in Mission where Najo lived (Seventh Street) was renamed "Leo Najo Street," and the Mission High School baseball stadium was also renamed in his honor.

Entrance to Najo Field (Photo by Noe Torres)

Early in the planning for the event, it was rumored that both U.S. President Richard Nixon and Mexican President Luis Echeverria might attend the event.

One of the organizers of the event told *The Mission Times*, "This will be a fine tribute to a man who has been a great credit to the game of baseball and to both his native and adopted countries."

During the celebration, many of Leo Najo's baseball friends and acquaintances gathered to pay him tribute. One of them, E. E. Marburger Sr. said, "It was my privilege to play baseball with and against Leo Najo both here and in Mexico. Looking back, Leo rates with the best outfielders. His one thing that stood above all other baseball players was his gracefulness in performing his duties. He made hard plays look easy." Marburger added, "I first met Leo in Tampico and played against him before he turned professional. Even as a youngster, he had the markings of a great player."

The local newspaper commented, "Leo Najo was the very soul of Mission's strong semi-pro team that was the rage of South Texas for decades. New stars would come along, but Najo kept playing, coaching, and managing. He has been an inspiration to young boys who look at him as an institution."

"Leo Najo had a very humble beginning," the article continued. "Though highly respected today, he is still a humble man. And he is grateful. He has always found time to help youngsters, at least in baseball, for baseball has been his life, and he had found all the time in the world to come out and help."

The 72-year-old Najo soaked in all the words and well wishes of his many admirers on that day in 1971. He spent time talking about the old times with his former teammates and other acquaintances. He sat and signed autographs for the many fans who requested it of him. It was a glorious day to be Leo Najo.

Leo's daughter Alicia recalls that her dad did not speak much about his baseball career late in his life. "Read about me in the record books," he told her. "Everything is there in the books."

On March 10, 1973, after having been selected by fans 34 years earlier, Najo became the first player formally inducted into the Mexican Baseball Hall of Fame at ceremonies held in Monterrey, Mexico. Najo's induction occurred at the unveiling of Mexico's first permanent Hall of Fame exhibit, a magnificent marble-trimmed building located on the grounds of the Cuauhtemoc Brewery in Monterrey. Cuahtemoc of Monterrey, coincidentally, was one of the first teams in Mexico that Najo played for, back in 1921. The Cuauhtemoc Brewery's involvement in baseball continues to this day, as the company owns Monterrey's team in the modern-day Mexican League. At the time of the Hall of Fame building's opening in 1973, the company had spent close to a quarter of a million U.S. dollars on the project.

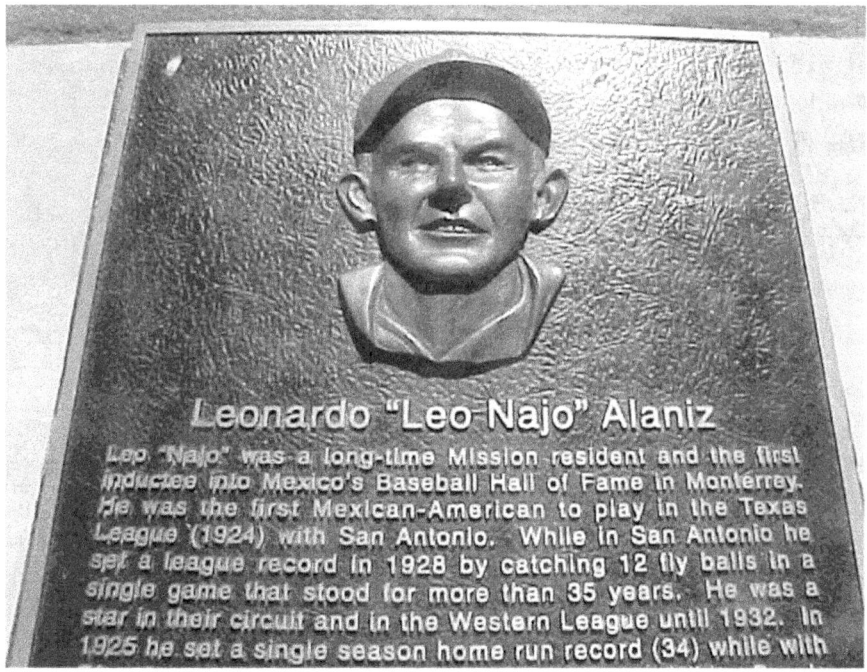

Plaque at Najo Field in Mission (2005 Photo By Noe Torres)

The 1973 ceremony was a grand occasion, and among those present was U.S. baseball commissioner Bowie Kuhn, as well as other representatives from American baseball.

Leo's wife, Elida, remembers vividly the family's trip to Monterrey, Mexico, for the induction ceremony. "We all went, and it was so beautiful and so emotional. We rode in a caravan of buses with an escort of police motorcycles with their sirens on."

At the hotel in Monterrey, she recalls that many reporters approached the group traveling with them to ask questions, and everyone but her husband seemed to talk freely about his exploits as a player. "I was getting anxious and wanted him to go tell the reporters something. I told him to go over there and say something." But Najo replied, "What am I going to say? I really don't have anything to add to what's already been written about me. My story is written in the record books for people to read, and sometimes when people say things later, they will add one or two extra things that aren't true. So, it's best just to leave it how it is written."

The induction occurred in the *Temple of Baseball Immortals*, where, flanked by a fountain on one side of the room and an eternal flame on the opposite side, bronze statues of Najo and the other Hall of Fame honorees were unveiled. A silver-plated inscription on each statue described that individual's baseball accomplishments.

Leo Najo's inscription reads: "LEONARDO (Najo) ALANIS (Mexican). Outfielder. In 1922, broke in with Mexico City and later joined the Aztecas. Made debut in Texas League in 1924 with San Antonio. Played in this circuit and in the Western League until 1932."

In 2005, the following expanded description of Najo's career appeared on the Mexican Baseball Hall of Fame's Web site:

"From 1924 to 1932, he was one of the best ballplayers in both the Texas League and the Western League. Idolized by San Antonio fans for his aggressive play and great skills, in 1928 he set a Texas League record by making twelve putouts in a single game from his position at centerfield

"He obtained the Western League's homerun title (34) in 1925 and batted .356 with 95 runs (record) for Okmulgee. In 1932, he hit the game-winning triple that gave Tulsa the championship. Back in 1926, he was purchased by the Chicago White Sox, but bad luck prevented his move to the major leagues. In a game for San Antonio, while fielding a fly ball, he collided with right fielder Pig Bodie and broke his leg.

"Najo debuted with Mexico City in 1922 with Cuauhtemoc of Monterrey, and his homerun led to a 1-0 victory over the Sonora team of Homobono Marquez, for whom he played many years later on the Aztecas.

LEO NAJO: BASEBALL'S FIRST LATINO SUPERSTAR

"In the Mexican League, he was player-manager for Tampico in 1939 and played briefly in 1941 with Mexico City. In Mission, Texas, where he resided, he was honored in many ways. In 1971, the city named the street where he lived in his honor, and also named the local high school's baseball field after him."

Najo was again honored in a Mexican Hall of Fame ceremony held on June 18, 1976. The occasion served to underscore how important a figure Najo was to fans of Mexican baseball history.

In 1975, Metro-Goldwyn Mayer studios contacted Leo about doing a motion picture based on his life and playing career. Although a film was never made, this event emphasizes what a large impact Najo had on baseball and on history. Leo's family still has a copy of the MGM contract that was offered to Leo for the rights to make the film of his life.

Leo Najo Gravesite (Courtesy of Alicia Farias)

Just as in the game of baseball, life inevitably has a final inning and a last out in the game. For Leo Najo, the end came on April 25, 1978 at the age of 79, after a battle with cancer and following gall bladder surgery. "Something went wrong during the surgery," his wife Elida remembers. "The surgery took longer than expect. Then they said he developed an infection."

Leo was survived by his wife, Elida Garza Alaniz; five sons: Leonardo, Jr., Rene, Jesse, Alberto, and Alfredo; and four daughters: Rosario, Alicia, Sylvia, and Linda.

His passing made national news. *The Sporting News* said, "Leo Najo, 78, a minor league outfielder in the 1920s and 1930s, died in Mission, Tex., recently. Najo, a native of Mexico, whose real name was Leo Alaniz, spent much of his 11-year playing career with San Antonio. Because of his speed and sharp fielding, he was the fans' favorite, and they were the ones who gave him the Najo name."

Even after his death, honors continued to come in for the incredible little center fielder from South Texas. Already inducted into the Mexican Professional Baseball Hall of Fame, Leo was posthumously inducted into the Rio Grande Valley Sports Hall of Fame, on April 7, 1988.

Year	*Team*	*Games*	*A-B*	*H*	*B.A.*	*P.O.*	*F.A.*
1924	S.A.	26	96	20	.208	27	--
1924	Tyler	108	392	150	.382	242	.992
1925	Okmulgee	142	559	213	.381	444	.977
1925	S.A.	2		2	--	9	--
1926	S.A.	82	290	90	.310	183	.976
1927	S.A.	122	390	115	.295	265	.976
1928	S.A.	158	581	161	.277	423	.967
1929	Omaha	120	421	133	.316	315	.979
1930	Omaha	129	471	168	.335	341	.975
1931	Omaha	92	334	119	.356	--	--
1931	S.A.	39	124	32	.266	34	1.000
1932	S.A.	33	129	31	.250	33	1.000
1932	Tulsa	113	427	138	.323	--	--
1938	McAllen	137	367	130	.354	229	.976

Leo Najo's Unofficial Composite Career Minor League Statistics

LEO NAJO: BASEBALL'S FIRST LATINO SUPERSTAR

In the year 2001, Minor League Baseball recognized Najo for his accomplishments while a member of the 1932 Tulsa Oilers of the Class B Western League. Najo is specifically mentioned as one of the reasons that Tulsa is ranked as one of the top 100 minor league baseball teams of the 20th century.

In the official records of Minor League Baseball, Leo is credited with ten years of experience in organized baseball (1924-32 and 1938). His years in Mexico do not count, as the Mexican League was not then part of the minor league system. In his ten years as a minor league player, he appeared in 1,177 games. He hit .323 with 99 homeruns, drove in 640 runs, and stole 209 bases.

In 1978, one of the first and one of the greatest Latino baseball players of the early 20th century left the earth. His spirit, however, lives on in everyone who knew him and everyone who hears his amazing story, which is why this book was written. Najo's story has been too long neglected and ignored by baseball historians and has remained generally unheard by the public. For a Latino in the 1920s to have overcome the obstacles Najo did and advance to where he was drafted and actually wore the uniform of a major league ball club was unprecedented. It is because Najo was such a remarkable player and such a wonderful person that so many South Texas residents remember him so fondly even today.

Every year since Leo's passing in 1978, a group of admirers, friends, and former teammates from throughout South Texas has gathered to remember the great Leo Najo. The "Najo Oldtimers Organization" became an official nonprofit organization in 2001, the year it celebrated its 30th anniversary. The group's mission is to preserve and honor the memory of Leo Najo and all the old-time ballplayers of South Texas.

On Saturday, October 1, 2005, an amazing 27 years after Najo's death, the 34th annual "Leo Najo Day" again drew hundreds of people to the Mission Community Center. Three weeks later, South Texas baseball fans watched in amazement as the major league team that drafted Leo Najo in 1925, the Chicago White Sox, won their first World Series since 1917 and, ironically, did so against a team from South Texas, the Houston Astros, a descendant of the old Texas

League team, the Houston Buffaloes, against whom Najo frequently played during his career.

Leo was 18 years old the last time the White Sox won the pennant, and seven years later, the Sox drafted him. Najo, who maintained a strong interest in major league baseball until his death, had a special fondness for Chicago and would surely have been pleased with the success of the 2005 White Sox team.

If a ghost truly does appear at Leo Najo Field in Mission, it was certainly smiling broadly after the 2005 World Series.

In 2019, the 48th Annual Leo Najo Day celebration was held at a new venue, the Mission Event Center, as it continued to grow and prosper in honoring the legacy of Leo Najo (Photo by Noe Torres).

Afterword
by Leo Najo's Granddaughter

Written by Athit Farias

I am amazed at the countless number of people whose lives my grandfather touched in one way or another. Almost everyone who knew him has a unique story to tell, some of which are incredible beyond belief. Here are just a few of my favorite remembrances of him.

A few years ago, my aunt Sylvia (Leo's daughter) went to Monterrey on business, and during a break, she and her daughter decided to visit the Mexican Baseball Hall of Fame. On the way to the Hall of Fame, the taxi driver asked what it was that attracted them to visit the baseball shrine. Sylvia told him that they were going specifically to view the exhibit about her father, Leo "Najo" Alaniz. The driver was overcome by sudden emotion and told my aunt that he had something very important to show her about her father. The man immediately pulled his cab over to the side of the road and asked Sylvia to step around to the rear of the vehicle.

As he opened the trunk of his cab, he showed my aunt a box that, as he later explained, contained all of his worldly possessions. Everything that was of value to him was in that box. The man opened his precious box, and near the very top, Sylvia saw a picture of the taxi driver as a child, standing next to Leo Najo. The driver said that, as a young boy, he idolized Leo Najo and would spend hours in the baseball stadium in Monterrey hoping to catch a glimpse of his hero. He would volunteer to help his father sell sodas at the games, in hopes of seeing the great Najo play ball. Closing his treasure box back up, he told Sylvia how much he treasured the picture of his hero and what an honor it was to meet her.

To me, Leo Najo was not just an outstanding ball player who racked up numbers, broke records, defied odds, and overcame racial barriers. I knew him as a very dedicated and caring family man. Most people knew "Najo" as the great baseball player, but I knew him as a doting grandfather who was always there for me. As an example of his thoughtfulness, I remember that at the slightest hint of cold in the air, he would rush to my school from his nearby home, bringing me a sweater to wear so that I would not be uncomfortable or get sick.

It wasn't until after his death that the extent of his baseball fame really came to light among most of my family members. I remember wondering why so many people attended his funeral, who they all were, and why there were so many reporters there. We did not fully understand until my grandmother sat us all down and explained that my Grandpa was actually a very famous baseball player both in Mexico and the United States and that he had accomplished great things in this professional baseball career. Still, this "Leo Najo" who everyone held in such high esteem as player was so incredibly different from the man I knew and loved.

The Leo Najo I knew would come driving up our street, honking his horn at his grandkids, and if you think an approaching ice cream truck attracts children, the sound of that Grandpa's car horn had an even stronger appeal to us. It caused all of us to drop what we were doing and charge toward him. We piled ourselves up on the hood of his car, like survivors clinging to a life raft, and he drove us slowly and carefully around the block toward his house, while we waved to passers-by. It was our daily parade in celebration of my grandfather.

As I was his only granddaughter for about a seven-year span near the end of his life, Grandpa showered me with special attention and called me his *Reina* (queen). As the queen of our daily parade, I always sat closest to the driver's side window, and my grandfather's long arm and big hand would reach out the window to hold me in place. I felt safe and secure with him. When the car reached its final destination, his house, we all jumped off and ran to him expectantly, knowing that he had a pocket full of caramel candies to share with us.

In another very pleasant memory, I remember that all of us grandkids would race to the kitchen table at his house to get the best seat for Grandpa's frequent magic shows. A talented amateur magician, he would hold us spellbound for hours with a few simple tricks. Sitting at the opposite end of the kitchen table from us, he often started his performance by taking a drinking glass and wrapping a newspaper tightly around it so that the newspaper took the shape of the glass. He then moved the wrapped glass in a circle above the table, while uttering a few choice "magic" words. Suddenly the glass would appear, unwrapped, in his lap below the table, and the only thing remaining in his hands was the empty newspaper, still retaining the shape of the glass.

Shortly before his death, he did this magic trick one last time, but with a special "twist" especially for me. He invited me to sit on his lap, as he performed his magic, and, of course, this vantage point allowed me to discover the secret behind the trick. While waving the covered glass around on top of the table, he worked it out of its newspaper wrapping and let it drop down into his lap. I remember looking at him when the glass fell on his lap, and he just grinned at me. An unspoken understanding passed between us, not just about what I had just seen, but also about many other memories we had shared. It was as if he knew that this performance would be his last, and he wanted to let me in on his "secret."

The really big secret that I never realized until after his death was exactly how much of an impact the game of baseball had on his life. There were, however, some clues. As a young girl, I was the typical tomboy and loved playing baseball and football with my cousins. I remember one day they refused to allow me to play with them because of my gender. I recall running to my grandparents' house in tears. My grandfather walked into the room and asked me why I was crying. I told him what had happened, and I'll never forget what he did next. He took hold of my chin with one of his large hands, looked me straight in the eye, and said in Spanish, "Don't you ever let anyone tell you that you can or can't do something because of who you are, whether it's because you're a girl or because you are Mexican."

Many years later, I understood that those words came from deep within my grandfather's heart, through the pain of all the discrimination he suffered as one of the first Latinos to play professional baseball. Knowing now what my grandfather endured during his playing days makes me appreciate so much more what he told me on that day. He had a way of planting "seeds" of knowledge that were designed to spring forth fruit for us much later in our lives. In retrospect, it is obvious to me how much his love of baseball and his own experiences as a player were passed along to all of us in his family.

A slogan that was popular some years ago -- "Baseball is life" – is nowhere truer than it is in my family. It was not easy being an Alaniz. Being born into the Alaniz family came with clear expectations with regard to athletic performance. Not only were we Alanizes expected to participate in sports, especially baseball, but also, we were expected to be the best at whatever sport we played. All of my cousins were tremendous baseball players. They were especially good pitchers, catchers, and base runners. One of my cousins could get to first base before the sound of the bat hitting the ball had dissipated.

The game of baseball was so important that it cost one of my cousins his sight in one eye. During a turn at bat in a high school game, he was struck in the eye by a wild pitch. Although he was told that he would never play baseball again, in true Alaniz fashion he proved everybody wrong. After weeks of determined practice, he learned to bat from the other side of his body so that he could track the progress of the pitches with his good eye. Not only did he finish the season with his high school team, but he also earned a baseball scholarship.

Success in baseball is so important in my family that it occasionally even transcends normal family loyalties. I remember a baseball game in which our local team's pitcher was having a terrible time. My grandmother kept yelling at the top of her lungs in Spanish for the struggling pitcher to be yanked from the game, when several embarrassed family members pointed out to her that the pitcher she was yelling about was family. Without missing a beat she replied, "Well, I know that, but he's terrible!" With her and my grandfather, there was no family favoritism when it came to winning.

I often wonder if somewhere deep in Leo Najo's psyche, being a part of a team was really a means of "belonging" to a group that could substitute for the family stability that he never experienced as a child. I say this with all respect for my great grandmother who raised him as a single mother. It was just the circumstances of the times in which Leo grew up.

I remember looking at my grandfather's legs and running my hands along the large bumps and knots of flesh on his shins, which (I learned years later) resulted from years of being stepped on and spiked while running the bases. As a child, I was intensely curious about what happened to his legs; however, out of respect and fear of hurting his feelings, I refrained from asking him about it. To this day, I recall vividly those terrible scars he carried to his grave.

After sustaining such brutal injuries, how could someone continue to play the game with such passion? How could he be so in love with a game that paid him so little and that caused him so much physical and emotional pain? Truly he must have loved the game, and truly he must have lived for being a member of a team. The pain was simply the price he chose to pay to be a part of the life he so enjoyed.

Still, even above baseball, family was the most important thing to him, and he made sure we all knew how important we were to him and to each other. When fights broke out among us, he invariably gave us a heartfelt scolding and reminded us that we should care and protect each other, not fight with each other. He said we were a "team" and impressed upon us the need to rely on each other and to look out for one another. Because of my grandfather's influence, to this day, our family remains a very close-knit group that takes care of its members who are in need. In my opinion, Leo Najo's greatest legacy is not what is written in a book of baseball records somewhere. It is not a bronze statue or plaque that recounts his many triumphs as one of the best ball players of the early 20th century. Leo's true legacy is his family, as well as the multitude of friends and admirers that remain loyal to him even so many years after his death.

And we are all convinced that somewhere, somehow, the great Najo still roams across fields of lush green grass, snagging fly balls dropping down from the heavens, and it is always a bright summer day ... and there is always hope of another championship season.

I love you Grandpa.

Bibliography

"After Ten Innings, the Bears Win, 6-5." *La Prensa* 17 Apr. 1924: 7.

Alaniz, Chayo. E-mail interview. 12 July 2005.

Alaniz, Elida. Personal interview. 1 Oct. 2005.

"Aviators Trim Packers, 6-0." *Valley Morning Star* 20 Mar. 1930: 4.

"Aztecas Administer Beating to San Antonio Bears." *La Prensa* 12 Sept. 1925: 8.

"Bears Beat the Cubs 4-0." *La Prensa* 14 Apr. 1927: 5.

"Batting Honors of Texas League Won By Carl Weis, Now With Cubs." *The Sporting News* 9 Oct. 1924: 6. *Paper of Record*. The Sporting News. 30 July 2005. Keyword: Houston.

"Biography: Leonardo Najo Alanis." *Hall of Fame of Mexican Professional Baseball*. 17 July 2005 <http://www.salondelafama.com.mx>.

"Box Score: Houston at San Antonio." *The Sporting News* 15 July 1926: 8.

"Calvo Establishes Fine Fielding Mark." *The Sporting News* 23 Oct. 1924: 8. *Paper of Record*. The Sporting News. 30 July 2005. Keyword: Antonio.

Cavazos, Jose M. Personal interview. Oct. 2005.

"Caught on the Fly." *The Sporting News* 23 Mar. 1933: 7. *Paper of Record*. The Sporting News. 30 July 2005. Keyword: Najo.

"Claiming of Drafted Players." *The Sporting News* 25 Feb. 1926: 8.

Clements, Bishop. "Des Moines and Packers Stage Circus." *Valley Morning Star*: 4.

Clements, Bishop. "Des Moines Defeats Omaha 13-8." *Valley Morning Star* 1 Apr. 1930: 4.

Clements, Bishop. "Des Moines Demons Rally to Win, 9-6." *Valley Morning Star* 21 Mar. 1930: 4.

Clements, Bishop. "Omaha Beats Denver 6-1." *Valley Morning Star* 6 Apr. 1930: 4.

Cook, Vic. "Valley Loop Extends Hand Across Border into Mexico." *The Sporting News* 30 Mar. 1939: 1. *Paper of Record*. The Sporting News. 31 July 2005. Keyword: Tampico.

"Cortinas Corrals Texas Valley Hitting Honors With .380 Mark." *The Sporting News* 24 Nov. 1938: 8. *Paper of Record*. The Sporting News. 31 July 2005. Keyword: Harlingen.

Crusinberry, James. "Collins Little April 1st Joke is Double Drill." *Chicago Daily Tribune* 2 Apr. 1926: 21. *Proquest*. Historical Newspapers. 19 July 2005. Keyword: najo.

Crusinberry, James. "Cubs and Sox to Test Out Flock of Shortstops." *Chicago Daily Tribune* 15 Dec. 1925: 26. *Proquest*. Historical Newspapers. 18 July 2005. Keyword: najo.

Crusinberry, James. "McCurdy, Recruit Sox Catcher, Must Beat Out Vet to Stick." *Chicago Daily Tribune* 3 Mar. 1926: 17. *Proquest*. Historical Newspapers. 18 July 2005. Keyword: najo.

Crusinberry, James. "Sox Drop Opener to Shreveport, 2-0; Cubs Win, 8-3." *Chicago Daily Tribune* 14 Mar. 1926, sec. A: 1. *Proquest*. Historical Newspapers. 18 July 2005. Keyword: najo.

Crusinberry, James. "Sox Play 5 Innings to Tie as Landis Leans on Head of Cane." *Chicago Daily Tribune* 4 Mar. 1926: 17. *Proquest*. Historical Newspapers. 18 July 2005. Keyword: najo.

Crusinberry, James. "White Sox Rope and Tie Texas Cowboys, 5 to 4." *Chicago Daily Tribune* 21 Mar. 1926, sec. A: 1. *Proquest*. Historical Newspapers. 18 July 2005. Keyword: najo.

Crusinberry, James. "White Sox Working into Pink in Red Hot Practice Games." *Chicago Daily Tribune* 17 Mar. 1926: 17. *Proquest*. Historical Newspapers. 18 July 2005. Keyword: najo.

"Demons Trounce Omaha 11-6." *Valley Morning Star* 22 Mar. 1930: 4.

Densa, Steve. E-mail interview. 18 July 2005.

De La Garza, Kika. Personal interview. 1 Oct. 2005.

"Denver Bears Victors Over Omaha, 13-10." *Valley Morning Star* 8 Apr. 1930.

"Denver Rallies in 10th to Win." *Valley Morning Star* 26 Mar. 1930: 4.

"Des Moines Loses 2 Tilts to Packers." *Valley Morning Star* 10 Apr. 1930: 4.

LEO NAJO: BASEBALL'S FIRST LATINO SUPERSTAR

"East Texas League Standing (1924 Season)." *The Sporting News. Paper of Record.* The Sporting News. July 2005.

Esser, Bruce. "Omaha." *Nebraska Minor League Baseball.* 18 July 2005 <http://marian.creighton.edu/~besser/baseball/wl1928.html>.

"Fans Ponder Probable Strength of Palms." *Valley Evening Monitor* 11 April 1938: 5.

Farias, Alicia A. Personal interview. 27 Aug. 2005.

Farias, Alicia A. Personal interview. 10 Sept. 2005.

Farias, Athit. Personal interviews. Aug. 2005.

Finger, Mike. "League of His Own: First Hispanic Star of S.A. Franchise." *San Antonio Express-News* 30 Apr. 2000, sec. C: 1+.

"Fox of Beaumont Champs Leads Texas League Batters With .357." *The Sporting News* 13 Oct. 1932: 6. *Paper of Record.* 29 July 2005. Keyword: Houston.

"Game Between San Antonio and Galveston Was Very Close." *La Prensa* 20 Apr. 1924: 15.

Garcia, Dario. Telephone interview. 26 Aug. 2005.

George, Harold K. "Omaha Has an Ailment Well Known to Others." *The Sporting News* 24 Apr. 1930: 3. *Paper of Record.* The Sporting News. 25 July 2005. Keyword: Omaha.

George, Harold K. "Omaha Has Hitting Punch." *The Sporting News* 9 Jan. 1930: 2. *Paper of Record.* The Sporting News. 25 July 2005. Keyword: Omaha.

"Giants and Omaha Play in Mission." *Valley Morning Star* 13 Apr. 1930: 7.

"Giants Beat Omaha 10-3." *Valley Morning Star* 16 Mar. 1930: 4.

Gillespie, Ray. "22 Slated for Induction to Mexican Shrine." *The Sporting News* 10 Mar. 1973: 73. *Paper of Record*. The Sporting News. 07 Aug. 2005. Keyword: Najo.

Goodale, George. "Injuries Fail to Stop Tulsa." *The Sporting News* 2 June 1932: 3. *Paper of Record*. The Sporting News. 29 July 2005. Keyword: Tulsa.

Goodale, George. "Tulsa Weighs Three Training Sites." *The Sporting News* 23 Feb. 1932: 2. *Paper of Record*. The Sporting News. 30 July 2005. Keyword: Najo.

"Houston and Ft. Worth Share Texas League Fielding Honors." *The Sporting News* 29 Oct. 1931: 6. *Paper of Record*. The Sporting News. 28 July 2005. Keyword: Wichita.

"Houston Beats San Antonio Yesterday Afternoon." *La Prensa* 13 Sept. 1925: 17.

Howe, Irwin M. "Hot Stove League." *The Washington Post* 8 Nov. 1925: 26. *Proquest*. Historical Newspapers. 18 July 2005. Keyword: najo.

"Indian Rookie, Bought by Sox, Burns Up League." *Chicago Daily Tribune* 15 Oct. 1925: 28. *Proquest*. Historical Newspapers. 18 July 2005. Keyword: najo.

"Jenkins of Wichita Falls, Gains Texas Batting Crown with .374." *The Sporting News* 21 Oct. 1926: 6. *Paper of Record*. The Sporting News. 22 July 2005. Keyword: Texas League.

LEO NAJO: BASEBALL'S FIRST LATINO SUPERSTAR

"Jensen and Keyes Monopolized Western League Hitting Honors." *The Sporting News* 27 Nov. 1930: 8.

"Jim Hudgens Hits .389 to Lead Western Association Batters." *The Sporting News* 19 Nov. 1925: 6.

Johnson, Lloyd, and Miles Wolff, eds. *Encyclopedia of Minor League Baseball*. 2nd ed. Durham, NC: Baseball America, Inc., 1997.

King, David. *San Antonio at Bat*. 1st ed. College Station, TX: Texas A&M UP, 2004.

Leo Najo Baseball Exhibit. 2005. Mission Historical Museum, Mission, TX.

"Leo Najo Day Set for Oct. 12." *McAllen Evening Monitor* 10 Oct. 1971.

"Leonardo Alaniz Najo Broke His Leg Yesterday Afternoon." *La Prensa* 8 July 1926: 8.

"Leonardo Alaniz, the Popular Najo, Arrived Yesterday." *La Prensa* 11 Sept. 1925: 10.

"Leonardo Leo Najo Alaniz." *City of Mission*. 17 July 2005 <http://www.missiontexas.us/lnajo.html>.

"L. Najo Will No Longer Play with San Antonio." *La Prensa* 6 May 1924: 7.

Miscellaneous San Antonio Bears Game Reports. *La Prensa* 1926.

Miscellaneous San Antonio Bears Game Reports. *La Prensa* 1927.

Miscellaneous San Antonio Bears Game Reports. *La Prensa* 1928.

Mission Celebrates Leo Najo Day. *Mission Times* 12 Oct. 1971: 1+.

Mosebach, Fred. "Rounding Up the Sports." *San Antonio Express* 9 August 1931: 12A.

"Najo and Schino Outfield Certainties." *The Sporting News* 16 Apr. 1931: 7.

"Najo Boasts Rapid Rise in Game." *The Washington Post* 19 Dec. 1925: 17. *Proquest*. Historical Newspapers. 18 July 2005. Keyword: najo.

"Najo Hits Home Run Number 34." *La Prensa* 30 Aug. 1925.

"Obituaries: Herrera." *San Antonio Express-News* 26 Feb. 2004. 23 Aug. 2005 <http://obits.mysanantonio.com>.

"Obituaries." *The Sporting News* 20 May 1978: 53.

"Oiled the Ways for Title in Western." *The Sporting News* 2 Nov. 1932: 7.

Oleksak, Michael M., and Mary A. Oleksak. *Beisbol: Latin Americans in the Grand Old Game*. 2nd ed. Indianapolis, IN: Masters P, 1996. 36-39.

"Omaha Beats Denver 7 to 2 in Mission." *Valley Morning Star* 30 Mar. 1930: 4.

"Omaha Defeats Denver 10 to 4 As Wind Blows." *Valley Morning Star* 25 Mar. 1930: 4.

"Omaha Defeats Mission 6 to 3 in Good Game." *Valley Morning Star* 18 Mar. 1930: 5.

"Omaha Pounds Out 6-5 Win Over Denver." *Valley Morning Star* 12 Apr. 1930: 4.

LEO NAJO: BASEBALL'S FIRST LATINO SUPERSTAR

O'Neal, Bill. *The Texas League 1888-1987: A Century of Baseball.* 1st ed. Austin, TX: Eakin P, 1987.

"Osborne Leads Texas Hitters with Mark of .432." *The Sporting News* 25 Sept. 1924: 6.

"Palms to Meet Harlingen at McAllen Today." *Valley Evening Monitor* 22 May 1938:6.

Pompa, Joe. Personal interview. 1 Oct. 2005.

Professional Baseball Player Database. Vers. 5.0. 18 July 2005 <http://www.baseball-almanac.com/minor-league/>.

Pullen, Michael A. "The Measure of a Man." *The Monitor* Sept. 1997.

"Raymond Ratcliff Ranks Best Among Batters of Texas League." *The Sporting News* 22 Oct. 1931: 8. *Paper of Record.* The Sporting News. 28 July 2005. Keyword: Wichita.

Rodriguez, Pikey. "Baseball oldtimers gather for Leo Najo Alanis Reunion." *The Brownsville Herald* 14 Oct. 2001. 17 July 2005 <http://www.brownsvilleherald.com>.

Ruggles, W. B. "Texas Reduces Player and All Salary Limits." *The Sporting News* 22 Oct. 1931: 3. *Paper of Record.* The Sporting News. 4 Sept. 2005. Keyword: Salary limit.

Ruggles, William B. *The History of the Texas League of Professional Baseball Clubs.* The Texas Baseball League, 1951.

"San Antonio Bears Win the First Game of the Season." *La Prensa* 15 Apr. 1926: 8.

"San Antonio Defeats Beaumont." *La Prensa* 21 Apr. 1924: 4.

Sanchez, Jesse. "Hall Honors Mexican Greats." *Major League Baseball News*. 7 Jan. 2004. 17 July 2005 <http://www.rstn.tv/NASApp/mlb/mlb/news/>.

Sanchez, Jesse. "History of Baseball in Mexico." *Major League Baseball*. 7 Jan. 2004. 19 July 2005 <http://mlb.mlb.com/NASApp/mlb/mlb/news/>.

"Santa Benson of Santone Arrives with Full Pack." *The Sporting News* 27 Dec. 1923: 3.

Saulsberry, Charley. "Tulsa Quick Win Jolts Club Pool." *The Sporting News* 22 Sept. 1932: 5. *Paper of Record*. The Sporting News. 30 July 2005. Keyword: Tulsa.

Scherwitz, Harold. "Honor for Leo Najo." *San Antonio Light* Oct. 1971.

Spalding_Official Base Ball Guide, 1929. Chicago; New York: A.G. Spalding & Bros., 1929. *Library of Congress*. 21 July 2005 <http://memory.loc.gov>.

Spalding_Official Base Ball Guide, 1930. Chicago; New York: A.G. Spalding & Bros., 1930. *Library of Congress*. 22 July 2005 <http://memory.loc.gov>.

Spalding_Official Base Ball Guide, 1939. Chicago; New York: A.G. Spalding & Bros., 1939. *Library of Congress*. 22 July 2005 <http://memory.loc.gov>.

Taylor, Sec. "Four Clubs in Western League Arrange a Separate Schedule." *The Sporting News* 23 Jan. 1930: 1. *Paper of Record*. The Sporting News. 28 July 2005. Keyword: Grande.

"Texas Fielding Averages." *The Sporting News* 3 Nov. 1927: 8.

"Texas Fielding." *The Sporting News* 13 Oct. 1932: 6. *Paper of Record*. The Sporting News. 29 July 2005. Keyword: Houston.

"Texas League." *The Sporting News* 21 Feb. 1929: 5.

"Texas League Notes." *The Sporting News* 23 Mar. 1933: 7.

"Texas League Standing - Game Reports - Notes (1924-1932)." *The Sporting News. Paper of Record*. The Sporting News. July 2005.

"Texas League Teams Are Ready For Season." *La Prensa* 16 Apr. 1924: 7.

Torres, Noe. *Ghost Leagues: Minor League Baseball in South Texas, 1910-1977*. Coral Springs, FL: Llumina P, 2005.

"Tulsans Going Home." *The Washington Post* 6 Mar. 1933: 11. *Proquest*. Historical Newspapers. 30 July 2005. Keyword: Najo.

"Turney, Righthander, to be on Mound for Palms." *Valley Evening Monitor* 14 April 1938: 8.

"Tyler Wins Lone Star Series." *The Sporting News* 11 Sept. 1924: 2.

United States. Bureau of the Census. Department of Commerce. *Fifteenth Census of the United States: 1930 Population Schedule*. 1930.

Valadez, Reynaldo. Personal interview. 1 Oct. 2005.

Vaughn, Irving. "Shortstop Only Real Problem on Hands of White Sox Boss." *Chicago Daily Tribune* 26 Dec. 1925: 13.

Proquest. Historical Newspapers. 18 July 2005. Keyword: najo.

Walsh, Bill. "A Tribute to the Late Leo Najo." *Valley Evening Monitor* 1971.

Weiss, Bill, and Marshall Wright. "Top 100 Teams: Team # 49 -- 1924 Okmulgee Drillers." 18 July 2005 <http://www.minorleaguebaseball.com/app/milb/history/>.

Weiss, Bill, and Marshall Wright. "Top 100 Teams: Team # 83 -- 1932 Tulsa Oilers." *Minor League Baseball*. 17 July 2005 <http://www.minorleaguebaseball.com>.

"Western Association Standing (1925 Season)." *The Sporting News* 1925. *Paper of Record*. The Sporting News. July 2005.

"White Sox Rookies Play Demons Here." *Valley Morning Star* 23 Mar. 1930: 6.

"Wichita Aviators Trim Giants 10-8." *Valley Morning Star* 18 Mar. 1930: 5.

"Wichita Aviators Win Flag As Season Comes to End." *Valley Morning Star* 16 Apr. 1930.

"Wichita Club in Western Loop Will Be Shifted to Tulsa, Okla." *The Sporting News* 4 Feb. 1932: 8. *Paper of Record*. The Sporting News. 28 July 2005. Keyword: Tulsa.

"With a 9-1 Score, the San Antonio Bars Win Game Three." *La Prensa* 19 Apr. 1924: 7.

Whitlock, Kelli. "Book Examines Baseball During the Depression Era." *Ohio University Research Communications*. 29 May 2002. Ohio University. 2 Sept. 2005 <http://news.research.ohiou.edu/>.

Wolff, Howard B. "Many Problems Facing Barney Burch This Season." *The Sporting News* 22 Jan. 1931: 5. *Paper of Record*. The Sporting News. 27 July 2005. Keyword: Omaha.

Wolff, Howard B. "Omaha Packers to Pack Heavy Bats This Season." *The Sporting News* 16 Apr. 1931: 7. *Paper of Record*. The Sporting News. 27 July 2005. Keyword: Omaha.

INDEX

Abbott, Spencer 73, 79
Ables, Harry T. 38, 48, 54
Adams, Carl 10
Alamo Peck Indians (San Antonio, Tx.) 7, 28
Alanis, Rosario (mother).... 1, 60, 127, 140
Alaniz, Chayo (daughter).. i, 127, 128
Alaniz, Elida Garza (wife) 24, 124, 125, 126, 127, 140, 148
Almada, Baldmero Melo ...... ii, 96
Alroy, Guy 112
Barrera, Pepe........ 4, 99, 102, 106
Beaumont, Texas . 14, 15, 40, 43, 49, 51, 55, 56, 82, 87
Bejerano, Agustin 120
Bell, James..................... 121, 122
Benson, Harry J. 19, 38
Bodie, Frank 43, 45, 138
Bowman, Abe 22
Bragana, Ramon 121
Broken leg (Leo Najo) 45, 48
Brought, Jimmy 28
Brown, Barney 120
Brownsville, Texas 2, 4, 5, 64, 109, 110, 111, 112, 116, 117, 130, 132, 133
Burch, Barney 58, 76, 79, 80
Byrd, William R............ 130, 131
Caldwell, Earl 4, 106
Carmona, Ernesto 121
Carrion, Jose Garza............... 106
Casas, Abelardo, Sr. 98, 105, 119
Castro, Angel 119
Castro, Joaquin 102
Cavazos, Jose M. 44

Cavazos, Meme 105
Chicago White Sox ii, 30, 31, 33, 34, 35, 36, 37, 38, 45, 47, 64, 72, 86, 96, 138, 141
Coleman, Bob........ 11, 14, 15, 16
Collins, Eddie 33, 34, 35
Comisky, J. Louis.................... 86
Contreras, Adan.................... 106
Contreras, Ernesto 102, 106
Corsicana, Texas 22
Couchman, Bob.................. 8, 51
Dallas Cowboys................. 4, 123
Davenport, Claude................... 10
De la Garza, Dario........ 4, 99, 106
De la Garza, Kika 4, 99, 100, 101, 104, 105, 106
De la Garza, Ramon 102
Dean, Dizzy............................ 75
Death of Leo's mother............. 60
Dihigo, Martin 118, 120, 121, 122
Dillard, Dan........................... 106
Donna, Texas............. 5, 130, 131
East Texas League 16, 19, 22, 35, 112
Echeverria, Luis (Mexican President) 136
Edwards, Monk 82
Estevis, Vicente.................... 134
Faber, Red 86
Farber, Red 67
Farias, Alicia (daughter)... iv, 11, 23, 108, 127, 129, 136, 140
Farias, Athit (granddaughter) . iii, 23, 24, 45, 124, 125, 129
Finger, Mike 22, 49
Flores, Erasmo...................... 101

LEO NAJO: BASEBALL'S FIRST LATINO SUPERSTAR

Flores, Ernesto 102, 105, 106
Fonsaca, Lew 86
Fort Worth, Texas 11, 35, 44, 55, 83, 87
Fractured shoulder blade 59
Friday, Ray 109, 112
Gallegos, Faustino 29
Galveston, Texas.. 12, 14, 15, 83, 87
Garcia, Dario. 100, 104, 105, 107
Garza, Matias 105, 106
Gibbs, Walton 105
Gibson, Frank 54, 113
Gonzales, Chano 102
Gonzalez, Jacinto 4, 99, 106
Gonzalez, Rodolfo 106
Grant, Julias 106
Great Depression ..iii, 62, 63, 73, 79, 94, 158
Greenville, Texas 21
Griggs, Art 86, 88
Gudat, Marv 28
Guerra, Manuel 106
Guerra, Porfirio 4, 99, 106
Harlingen, Texas 64, 109, 112, 113, 114, 116, 131, 132, 133
Hausman, George 111
Herrera, Lucia 58, 63, 124
Homerun Leader, Western Association 29
Houston, Texas 15, 19, 29, 39, 43, 44, 51, 54, 56, 57, 87
Indian (References to Najo) ... 10, 29, 30, 31, 33, 36
Jackson, George 22
Jefferson, Bill 122
Johnson, Paul 106
Jordan, Kirby 113
Kitchens, Frank 19, 22
Kopp, Wally 112
Kuhn, Bowie .... ii, 137

La Lajilla, Mexico 1, 93
Landis, Kenesaw Mountain.. ii, 34
Landry, Tom 4, 104, 105, 123
Laredo Apaches 130, 131
Laredo, Texas.2, 6, 13, 101, 116, 130, 131, 132, 133
League Park (San Antonio, Tx.) 7, 11, 12, 42, 49, 55, 87
Legion Park (McAllen, Tx) 66
Lehman, Lyndal 106
Leo Najo Day (1971) 135
Leo Najo Street (Mission, Tx.) 135
Lopez, Rene 105
Los Angeles Times 48
Lower Rio Grande Valley League 64, 72
Lutteroth, Salvador 121
Lyons, Ted 87
Mack, Connie 5
Madero, Texas 107
Marburger, Eddie 106, 136
Marquez, Homobono 6, 138
Marshall, Dewey 10
McAllen Palms 109, 110, 111, 112, 113, 114
McAllen, Texas 5, 36, 64, 98, 100, 106, 109, 110, 111, 112, 113, 114, 116, 123, 130
McClanahan, Campbell 112
McGrew, Slim 10
Melch, Herb 106
Mercedes, Texas 5, 115
Metro-Goldwyn Mayer ... iii, 139
Mexican Baseball Hall of Fame .... iii, 6, 120, 136, 138, 140
Mexico City.. 116, 117, 120, 121, 122, 138, 139
Milmo Bank team (Laredo, Tx.)6
Mission (Tx.) High School 135

Mission 30-30 (*La Treinta Treinta*) Team 4, 5, 65, 95, 96, 98, 99, 100, 101, 102, 104, 105, 106, 107, 108, 122, 130, 133, 134
Mission 30-30 Stadium 98
Mission Historical Museum 2, 95, 105, 123
Mitze, Carl 38, 51
Monterrey, Mexico ..... iii, 6, 101, 116, 122, 136, 138
Moreno, Enrique 105
Najo Oldtimers Organization 141
Najo, Origin of Nickname 4
Negro Leagues 120
New York Giants 65, 66, 72
New York Yankees 8, 114
Night baseball 73, 76, 79
Nixon, Richard M. (President) 136
Okmulgee, Oklahoma 25, 26, 27, 29, 30, 31, 138, 140
Old-timers game (1957) 135
Omaha, Nebraska. 58, 59, 60, 61, 64, 68, 71, 73, 74, 75, 76, 77, 78, 79, 80, 81, 82, 83, 89, 93
Our Lady of Guadalupe Church (Mission, Tx.) 1, 2
Pasquel, Jorge 121
Pena, Bernardo 8, 102
Pena, Taurino 4, 99, 106
Philadelphia Athletics 5
Pinon, Ines 105
Pittsburgh Pirates .. 64, 69, 72, 86
Pompa, Eliseo 107
Pompa, Joe 13, 43, 103, 104, 105, 107, 155
Puente, Jose 105
Radio broadcast, first 114
Ramirez, Gonzalo 11, 60, 63, 101
Ramirez, Luisa (sister) 60, 63

Record 12 putouts in one game 55
Reese, Andy 65
Released by Chicago White Sox 36
Retirement from Organized Ball (1933) 94
Rickey, Branch 4, 54
Rio Grande Valley League ... 109, 130, 131, 132, 133
Rio Grande Valley Sports Hall of Fame 140
Rodriguez, Camilo (teammate) 45, 107
Rodriguez, Guayule 101, 105
Ruth, Babe 8
Saenz, Jesus 4, 99, 106
Saenz, Jose 4, 99, 106
Salazar, Lazaro 120
San Benito, Texas 5, 64, 115
Sanchez, Eduardo 105, 107
Sanchez, Santos 107
Scherwitz, Harold 6, 11, 45
Seabough, J. Warren ... 29, 30, 31, 32
Segovia, Tereso 102
Shivers, Allan (Texas governor) 104
Shreveport, Louisiana. 33, 34, 35, 42, 49, 51, 54, 55, 83, 87
Signing by San Antonio, 1923 10
Smith, Herb 79
Smith, Theolic 122
Solis, Rene 107
St. Louis Cardinals .4, 36, 54, 75, 76
Strohmeyer, George 4, 107
Tampico, Mexico 6, 116, 117, 118, 119, 120, 130, 136, 139
Tavern (the 30-30 Bar) in Mission, Tx.. 95

Taylor, Ray 114
Texarkana, Texas 35
Texas League . ii, 2, 8, 10, 11, 12, 16, 25, 29, 34, 35, 36, 37, 42, 48, 49, 53, 55, 82, 83, 85, 86, 88, 94, 99, 135, 138, 157
Texas Valley League ... 109, 114, 115, 116, 117, 118, 119
Tising, Jack 22
Topeka, Kansas.... 58, 59, 74, 77, 80, 82
Trautman, George M 132
Treda, Joe 4, 99, 106
Tulsa Oilers ii, 59, 60, 85, 86, 88, 89, 90, 91, 92, 93, 94, 95, 98, 135, 138, 141
Tyler, Texas ... 16, 18, 19, 21, 22, 25

University of Texas at Austin 123
Valadez, Rey . 105, 106, 134, 157
Vasquez, Jose 105
Vela, Pedro I 4, 99, 106
Veltman, Pat 36
Wachtel, Paul 10
Waco, Texas ... 38, 39, 42, 48, 49, 54, 55, 56
Walsh, Billy 106
Washington Post .... ii, 30, 31, 94, 109
Weslaco, Texas 5, 106, 131
Western Association 25, 31, 72
Wetzel, Frank 58, 61
Woods, Bill 105
Wright, Perry 106
Yoder, Bill and Nick 107
Yowell, Carl 22

Check Out the Author's Other Books!
Available at RoswellBooks.com

Long before the first airplane took flight, when nothing but birds should have been in the skies, the early residents of the United States witnessed bizarre unidentified flying objects of all sizes, shapes, and descriptions. They encountered strange beings that clearly were not human, including "Men in Black" and possibly time travelers. They saw huge motherships, underwater UFOs, and other unexplained wonders. Some of America's most famous early historical figures, including Thomas Jefferson, Ben Franklin, George Washington, shared an interest in UFOs and extraterrestrials. Contained within these pages is the "other" American History that you were never taught in school!

The Real Cowboys & Aliens: Early American UFOs by Noe Torres & John LeMay is available in print and for the Kindle at RoswellBooks.com and through online retailers including Amazon.com. Scan the QR code above to order your copy from Amazon today!

UFO expert Nick Pope says, "If you think the UFO mystery began in 1947 with flying saucers and the Roswell crash, think again. This fascinating, data-rich book explores a wealth of intriguing incidents that were formerly interpreted through the lens of folklore, but which could now lead to a fundamental reappraisal of the greatest mystery of the modern age. With the focus on the 19th century, this delightful tome shines a light on a slice of American history that shows truth really can be stranger than fiction."

Best-selling author Donald Schmitt says, "What Torres and LeMay have clearly defined in this suspenseful thriller tome, is that the UFO accounts portrayed throughout this exhaustively researched work, remain in a separate class…. Aside from a rare hot-air balloon or dirigible, there was nothing else in the air back then… or on the ground; the witnesses are clearly describing something which precedes the Wright Brothers technology."

Many other books from Noe Torres are available at his web site, RoswellBooks.com.

www.ingramcontent.com/pod-product-compliance
Lightning Source LLC
Chambersburg PA
CBHW050639300426
44112CB00012B/1858